Don't Let Fear Paralyze You

A Guide To Your Own Personal Freedom

by Michael Challenger

DON'T LET FEAR PARALYZE YOU

Don't Let Fear Paralyze You – A Guide to Your Own Personal Freedom
Registration No.: 1136156

Canadian Intellectual Property Office | An Agency of Industry Canada
© 2017 Michael Challenger
www.michaelchallenger.com

Disclaimer

This book contains the ideas and opinions of its author. The intention of this book is to provide information, helpful content and motivation to readers about on the subjects addressed. It is shared and sold with the understanding that the author is not engaged to render any type of psychological, medical, legal or any other kind of personal or professional advice. No warranties or guarantees are expressed or implied by the author's choice to include any of the content in this volume. The reader should always consult his or her medical, health or other professional and accredited health provider before adopting any of the suggestions in this book or drawing any ideas, inferences or practices from this book. The author shall not be liable for any physical, psychological, emotional, financial or commercial damages, including, but not limited to, special, incidental, consequential or other damages. The reader is responsible for their own choices, actions and results.

1st Edition, 1st printing 2017

Cover design by: Kriste Vinet (www.teniv.ca) and
Michael Challenger (www.anu-entertainment.com)

Interior design by: Steve Walters at
Carolyn Flower International (www.carolynflower.com)
and Kriste Vinet

Author photo by: Edward Aninaru

Biography Picture: John Bregar

ISBN-13: 978-1540340795 (CreateSpace-Assigned)
ISBN-10: 1540340791

Endorsements

"A wonderfully insightful, practical and motivating guide to making transformational change in one's life. Michael communicates beautifully a very real and accessible road map to tapping into your true potential through letting go of fear based thoughts and behaviours. The content is incredibly authentic and inspiring and will put you on the path to connecting with your absolute best self. This book is a must read!"

Greg Klym
Mindfulness – Meditation Yoga Teacher

"What an incredible, inspiring and transformational book that pushes you to push past your fears and limitations. Thank you Michael for sharing this blueprint for personal mastery."

Kim Thomas
Educator, Motivational Speaker, Wellness Coach

"If fear is the dragon standing in your way, Michael Challenger's book *Don't Let Fear Paralyze You!* is the secret weapon that slays that dragon for good. Each chapter provides insights and practical tips as well as an illustration throughout to encourage the reader to pause for a breathe in order to re-align and re-evaluate. A really wonderful authentic guide to your own personal freedom."

Carolyn Flower
Bestselling author of Gravitate 2 Gratitude - Journal Your Journey

"*Don't Let Fear Paralyze You!* is a must read for anyone that's on their journey to self-discovery. Especially for anyone that's been exposed to a very dark place within the "Fear" based experience. Michael Challenger has faced his own fears head on and has provided some insights on how to unlock the code to self-advancement."

Pauline Christian
President of the Black Business and Professional Association

"A mind that is stretched by a new experience can never go back to its old dimensions."

Oliver Wendell Holmes, Jr.

Dedication

To my one and only true mentor who inspires me each day: my mother, Paulette Theresa Challenger, a warrior with a heart of gold and the compassion of Mother Teresa. I truly don't know how I could have done any of this without your continuous love and support.

I count my blessings every day and give many thanks for being your son. You continue to inspire me with your hard work and determined spirit to succeed in life. Your backbone of love and strength helps me day after day and I truly thank you from the bottom of my heart.

Your son, your only son…;)

Michael

"True success is
overcoming the
fear of being
unsuccessful."

Paul Sweeney

Don't Let Fear Paralyze You - A Guide To Your Own Personal Freedom

"When the going gets tough, get stronger."

Michael Challenger

Preface

This book emerged from looking at myself in the mirror and understanding what my role in this lifetime is truly meant to be. I wrote this book because I looked fear in the face and came out stronger. Now I want to help others break the chains that wrap around their minds and bodies and prevent them from achieving greatness. The chains that tell us we're not good enough in life left me no choice: I was compelled to share how my life changed after I found the strength to conquer the fear that had dictated my entire existence.

This book was written and developed for people who are done with living mediocre lives and want to make significant changes. I wanted to create a tool that can either remind you of the power you already possess or give you a simple boost whenever you're down.

When you genuinely know you're taking the necessary steps in fulfilling your happiness, nothing and no one can deter you from achieving what truthfully belongs to you. As some of you may already know, the only person that's stopping you is ultimately you.

Knowing that you or I can contribute the smallest thing in life, whether it's acknowledged or not, it can and will make a difference. Don't ever let anyone stop you from being you; if your heart is telling you, 'this is who I am', then you must trust it and listen.

Let this first page be a wake-up call to your dreams. If you feel alone, just know that I'm here to remind you that you are great. Yes, we may never meet or speak to one another, but I have your back 100 per cent and believe in you. I really mean that.

Each of these chapters are part of the fear puzzle and by giving each chapter an inner glimpse we can overcome the fear that paralyzes you by breaking one chain link at a time.

Throughout this book your going to see this symbol.

Every time it appears I'd like to suggest you pause and breathe. Breathe in and breathe out then continue with your reading.

Peace and blessings,

Michael Challenger

"The most beautiful people we have known are those who have known defeat, known suffering, known struggle, known loss, and have found their way out of the depths. These persons have an appreciation, sensitivity, and an understanding of life that fills them with compassion, gentleness, and a deep loving concern. Beautiful people do not just happen."

Elisabeth Kübler-Ross

Chapter One
Kicking Fear In The Ass

Fear

Do you constantly fear the next step? Do you make your choices out of fear? Do you let other people make decisions for you because you're afraid to make a mistake? You may answer yes to all of these questions, or maybe just one or two. Regardless, this book was written in hope that one day you can push past your fears and achieve whatever you want in life.

This book was created to help you change yourself, change your destiny... open up to new ways of thinking and make changes that result in a better version of yourself.

"An unpleasant emotion caused by the belief that someone or something is dangerous, likely to cause pain, or a threat."

Fear is a natural physiological defense mechanism that we all have in order to let us know whether something or someone may be dangerous to us. However, over the years many of us have acquired irrational fears based on past experiences and because of that, we talk ourselves out of doing things before we even begin.

What I've come to realize is that people who don't challenge themselves enough end up frustrated with the offerings of life. When fear completely takes over, you not only become frustrated with your environment, you ultimately become frustrated with yourself.

DON'T LET FEAR PARALYZE YOU

Greatness blocker

Yes, we all have certain physiological fears embedded within us that function to keep us safe. But at the same time, fear is the biggest greatness blocker there is. It prevents you from living the life you were meant to live. Getting past your fears, one at a time, will build strength and confidence inside you.

Your intuition is your connection to your inner truth. When we're unsure or afraid to confront the things that paralyze us in life, the power of the universe can't provide us with the support we need to move forward. Opening ourselves up to our own truth helps us continuously evolve and grow. New life experiences will be waiting around every corner once you become open to them. Once you let your greatness in, who knows what you're capable of? You won't know until you get there. Now, if that's not something to look forward to, I don't know what is!

So if you're ready to face your fears and take action, keep reading!

So the question is how do we kick fear the ass?

You have to be completely honest with your cycles of emotions and be aware of the things that keep coming up from within. If you're unclear and can't grasp onto your fears, then you need to reach out and seek support – perhaps faith-driven spiritual guidance, a support group or professional help – to help steer you in the right direction.

When I was blocked from moving forward, I took it seriously – and so should you. It's your time to rise up and make the best out of your current situation, without holding back. I've never completely understood the stigma that some communities or people have about seeking professional help. There's nothing wrong with it and if you're too shy to seek help through the medical system, find online chats, Skype with a coach, find a mentor and discuss your concerns in private. Remember, you're the only one who can stop you from being great. There's absolutely no better feeling in the world than to kick fear in the ass and create your best possible life.

Here's an example of one of the things that stifled me from moving forward in life: speaking in public used to terrify me. My situation was complex; I was always full of energy around people (nothing has changed, believe me),

6

yet I suffered from a major lack of confidence when speaking in front of a group of people. I suffered from Glossophobia; a severe fear of public speaking. Also, in general, I would always put other people's happiness before my own. In other words, I had the disease to please and conveniently forgot to work on the things that needed focus.

Let's look at some of the reasons why fear came into my life, and may come up in yours.

What's stopping you?

We often make things harsher in our heads than they actually are. If you tell yourself that you'll do it when all the conditions are right, then you may be waiting forever, and forever is too late.

Instead, ask yourself what is it that you want out of life and when would you like to achieve it? Then ask yourself what it would take for you to get there.

Whatever comes up for you, please write it down

_____

_____

_____

_____

_____

_____

If it feels too hard to get what you want, somewhere inside you there are certain fears that are stopping you from moving forward, always delaying or postponing. We sometimes try to be perfect and wait for the perfect conditions – but none of us are perfect nor will we ever be. And believe me, perfect conditions do not exist. It's all about the journey. Procrastination is also another way for us to stay comfortable within our discomfort. I remember the first time I heard a quote about jumping off a cliff and building your wings on the way down; it felt like a direct message to me. I can gladly say that I now live by that quote every day. It's been a wild ride, but I wouldn't go back and change it for anything in the world!

You can choose to break down your fears into more manageable parts and work through them, or you can do it the way I did and look fear directly in the face. But you must know what it is you fear, deep down inside. If you don't know what you're afraid of, how can you hope to work through your fears?

Re-examining yourself

First thing, don't beat yourself up. Take the time to re-examine yourself and look at some of the things that need shifting. Investing in counselors and therapists definitely help, but most of the time they don't go deep enough. How can they? You're essentially in charge of your own happiness. So be gentle and patient with yourself. Things you were doing in the past worked out well and got you this far; now look at what's not working and take it from there. One of the most important things you can ask yourself is in what area of your life do you feel unhappy. Maybe you've been tolerating a miserable situation for so long that you've become numb. If you can't feel anything at all, then please get help. I promise you that if you're determined to beat it and get ahead, you will. You will always get through the stormiest of times – you just need to figure out what areas of your life most need to change.

Ask yourself the following questions and take note of the FIRST thing you feel after every question. All I want you to do is notice whether you feel primarily good or bad. Please circle the corresponding feelings. Do this for every question.

How is my home life? Is it comfortable there? Do I have everything I need?

Good   Mixed   Bad

Do I love my job? Do I make enough money for what I need? Do I make more than enough money for the things I want? Does my job challenge me in ways that force me to grow and expand as a person? Is there room for a promotion or advancement?

Good   Mixed   Bad

What about my health? Do I take good care of myself – eat well, sleep well and exercise enough? Do I eat healthy foods that I know will nourish my body?

Good   Mixed   Bad

Relationships? Do I feel loved? Supported? Do I have a significant other in my life? And if so, is he or she the right one?

Good   Mixed   Bad

What does my social life look like? What kind of friends do I have?

Good   Mixed   Bad

My spiritual connection. How do I feel about my spiritual and personal development?

Good   Mixed   Bad

Take time and really think about the areas in which you felt more bad than good and work on the things that need changing. You have full control over all of the things we just discussed; your home life, your work, your health, your love life and your social life. It might not always seem that way, but it's the truth. Whether the choice was direct or indirect, you live it every day. This is about figuring out who you are, who you've been, and who you would like to become.

For years I didn't quite grasp the saying, "There is nothing to fear but fear itself." I didn't get it until I tried living it. The choice is yours. How will you direct your energy in life?

Known and unknown fears

We're all familiar with common phobias like arachnophobia, the fear of spiders; claustrophobia, the fear of being in tight spaces, and then there's acrophobia which is a fear of heights. Many people seem to suffer from that last one. Where do these fears come from? Why do some people have them while others don't? One person can be terrified of a spider, while others will pick it up with their bare hands and place it outside without fear. How can one person feel one way and the other person another? I truly think it's all based on our belief system and how we're taught. If you accept that a spider is potentially harmful because you've heard stories, then that's what you'll believe. You've just created another fear by choosing to believe in the possible negative outcome of any given situation. Maybe it started because someone you trusted told you that spiders were dangerous. Their reasoning sounded good to you, so you chose to believe them. This is quite different from having past experiences that left you feeling afraid and not wanting to revisit the things that scared you in the first place. Let's call them our "underlying fears."

How do you get to a place of knowing what you don't currently know? This is what Einstein was referring to when he discussed "reaching another level of consciousness." Consciousness is another word for awareness. Einstein said that "we can't solve our problems at the same level of consciousness that created them." The first step to getting anywhere or learning anything is to remain open-minded.

Open-mindedness

One definition of being open-minded is taking courageous steps towards a happiness that you may have never known. A courageous person stays open, no matter what fears may arise along the way.

Some people need to have full control of everything in their lives in order to feel safe. Others would rather take the risk of uncertainty, and quite possibly lose a little control in order to evolve and have a new experience or outlook in life. Which camp are you in right now? Do you believe in things that can't be proven? Or are you willing to follow your gut and focus on the things that matter most to you.

Opening your heart

Please consider what I'm about to say. Give others a chance to influence you in a positive way. When we close our minds, it's most likely due to anger or negative experiences that have not yet healed. Try remaining open in every way and be smart about your life. Use all of your senses, including common sense, to develop the different steps and stages in your life.

Let's say you're open about learning and ready to face your darkest fears. Break them down first if you need to – we each have our own set of fears that is unique to us alone. This has become a part of who we are and how we function as individuals in society. A vast majority of people are afraid to do what they really would like to do in life and need a strong desire for change and enough emotional energy to make it happen.

Breaking it down

Fear is a feeling. Nothing more, nothing less. The amount of fear you feel or don't feel is due to how much energy you feed into it. We all have different kinds of fear. Each one of your fears has a certain amount of 'fear energy' starting with your thoughts. It always starts there.

The less you think about the thing that keeps coming up, the less energy and power you're feeding into it. If you don't want it, don't think about it. It's that simple. Not easy I know, but try focusing on what you want in life, rather than what is absent.

The objective is to get to a place where you truly love yourself and get closer to your intuition – that is what deciphers your truth in this lifetime. You'll start becoming your own best friend and paving the course that is meant for you to lead. If you feel you have nothing at all right now, just be patient and continue to have hope.

Integrity and morals

Integrity is a word we hear all the time and many of us think we have a good comprehension of the word, but do we really? The layman's definition for integrity is simply adhering to a set of principles or moral rules and being honest. The amount of integrity you have is determined by how much you stick to your principles. I think we consider people of integrity to be 'solid' or 'sound' people. We could say someone with integrity is a person who adheres to certain beliefs or rules of conduct that could be considered righteous. What does integrity mean to you and how much of it do you have? Are you someone who values truth, honesty, and doing the right thing? What types of things do you personally accept or condemn? How do you try and show up in the world – or how would you like to?

Face it! Demystifying the unknown

What is your fear? The only way to get beyond it is to walk through it. There's no quick fix or ways around this one. Of course, how you do it will determine how easy or difficult it will be for you. The part of fear that scares us the most is the element of the unknown. Either you own your fears or they own you. If you get close enough to any of your fears, can you be somewhat objective about them? You'll soon learn that when the unknown becomes known, the fear is automatically eliminated.

The unknown might present a certain element of fear, but what would life be without it? There will always be an element of the unknown in everything based on free will. Nothing is pre-determined and life is forever changing. Surely, you've heard of "no pain, no gain." That's a concept I've pondered for many years. I've come to understand the nature of its origin is about the ride and enjoying it. In other words, the real reward is in what you did to get to where you are.

You can do it!

Tackling your fears can seem like a giant stack of 'to-do's' before you break it down into something manageable. But you will feel differently after you tackle a couple and get to the other side. I can't tell you how you will feel; I can only tell you that you will start to feel better. Once you've tackled one fear, tackling other fears becomes easier. You work your way up. You won't even be aware of some fears until later on, after getting to another level of understanding. *It's about being willing to do the work.* New things become less scary when they're no longer new to us. Claim your power. Take your place in this world and do something special for yourself. How else will you find out what it is if all you do is sit on the sidelines and watch everyone else around you succeeding in life? You have to participate in life; it's not just a spectator sport. Much can be said about learning, but doing is just as important. If you get stuck, put a pin in it with a return deadline. Don't leave the important things open to chance. You can do anything if you're determined enough to accomplish it. **ANYTHING**

The other side of FEAR – an abundant world

We live in a world of abundance. There is more than enough of everything to go around and then some. Conquering fear is about expansion and spreading our wings. We're all striving for more these days and not doing enough to get what we deserve. Operating from a place of mental scarcity diminishes our chances of abundance within the universe. If you're in scarcity-thinking mode, please continue to work on the necessary changes and ask for what you deserve. Part of the process is being aware of your feelings with each new experience. Allowing your mind to be free is a big part of that process , open up and work on the receiving part of your life.

Additional Notes:

_____

_____

_____

_____

_____

_____

_____

_____

_____

_____

_____

_____

_____

_____

_____

_____

_____

"If you don't like it,
change it!"

Michael Challenger

Chapter Two
Trust Your Power

Power

The amazing thing about having your own unique story is that you have the power to share your vision with family, friends, local communities or even millions of people in the world. The power we all possess can truly change the world. No matter how small you think your idea or action may be, your support in any given situation can change the course of someone else's life.

Helping other people has always been the number one thing that comes naturally to me and still excites me today. At a recent business meeting I attended, someone asked the group to remember what they wanted to be when they grew up. As a child, I honestly never had an answer to that question. In retrospect, I believe I was too busy learning about life and taking everything in. As I grew older, I just followed my heart, which led me to becoming the person that I am today. Every day, I choose to follow my spirit and heart in any given situation. I sometimes make a choice out of a pure gut feeling; other times, I make sure my eyes are wide open and assess the given situation. Nevertheless, I'm amazed with my life and the protection I've received along the way.

An aside: this is my first book and it comes straight from the heart. If it helps you transform in any way, then I'm truly honored and will be forever grateful. Nothing in life makes me happier. Sincerely.

It takes time

In the world in which we live everything moves so fast that we forget to slow down and work steadily towards the dream. The only way to truly measure one's success is through dedication and time. If you think you don't have to prove anything and showing up is enough, you're wrong. Successful people work hard every day and continue to prove their worth to the people around them and ultimately to themselves. Regardless of how much you have or don't have right now, your enlightened self will know if you deserve the type of success you're seeking. When you wake up with appreciation and take the time to accept everything around you, you will have created your own version of success. It's not about what other people want for your happiness, it's what you know to be true for yourself.

Is it hard to be consistent and make efforts every day?

Yes. Is your situation more difficult than your next-door neighbor? Maybe, but at the end of the day, comparisons and self-pity won't change the situation. No matter how green it looks on the other side of the fence, everyone faces challenges . The only way for you to move forward is by being consistent and committing to your happiness – that is the ultimate victory. When you sit down and get serious about what it will take, be real about your given situation. If you're serious about your dreams, then you don't need to worry about it, you'll get there.

Steps

The most important thing in life is to focus on the steps it takes to achieve your goals. The whole purpose of feeling great or celebrating your achievements is to be aware of the efforts you made to get there. We all admire the greats because they achieved their individual goals and are successful at what they do. The amount of work and effort it takes for people to achieve their goals in life is truly phenomenal, especially when one learns about the behind-the-scenes circumstances of their lives.

Plan

You need to plan things out first and get clear about your goals so that eventually you'll experience everything your heart desires. Going out with friends and getting drunk twice a week or lying on the couch watching television for long hours every day may be something you need to reconsider in order to achieve your goals. If you need to be the first person in your family who gets up earlier than everyone else in the house, then it may be something you need to consider doing if you want to get to where you want to be in life. Yes, leisure and R&R is highly recommended, but prioritizing and overall discipline has to become one of your priorities.

I like talking about taking appropriate steps because most people, including myself, don't always want to be patient; we get angry, bored, anxious, tired, overwhelmed etc. But when we take the right steps, the gratification we get when looking back is extremely satisfying and can almost guarantee you'll be happy with yourself in the end. Hard work is not something that is taken lightly in the world. If someone sees the time and effort or passion you put into something, the universe will reward you with the right type of message, and support.

Here's an example that blows my mind:

A very good friend of mine has a goal: to be one of the best soccer coaches in Canada. It all started with a vision, but with no real substance to support the end result. He opened up his life by resolving to work towards his happiness. His determination allowed him to quit his job, step away from his beautiful condo and moved into his parent's basement. In other words he restarted his life from scratch. Now that's somebody committed to change. When he went through these steps and reflected on the change, even he – and perhaps many of his friends – thought he was absolutely crazy at the time. However, looking back and witnessing the type of progress he's made, it was completely the right thing to do. Within the first two years of taking those steps, he transformed his situation and rebuilt himself. Since then, he's been juggling jobs within his field, got a new place, left a very dysfunctional relationship and took action towards attaining his dreams. This man is one of my dearest friends and I know he and I will soon be celebrating his dreams having become a reality.

Your vision comes from the heart and nothing else. Unfortunately, the negative voices inside your head will often try to steer you away from your greater self.

DON'T LET FEAR PARALYZE YOU

How familiar is this to you?

Friend: Hey, how are things moving along with your goal?

You: Great! Things are fine!

The truth is:

a) Your life and responsibilities take the best of you and you step away from the dream, promising yourself that one day you'll be back.

b) Your real job only gives you 20% of your time towards your goal.

c) You realize that the journey towards your goal is a lot harder than you anticipated. Now your confused, wondering if this dream is what you really want.

d) You find every excuse in the book, explaining why it's no longer possible for you to achieve the dream.

There's a ton of other excuses or reasons out there that I'm not listing. The question you need to ask yourself is: are you ready to trust your own power and do whatever it takes to achieve your goal? Do you believe that even if it's seems really hard, can you trust yourself to do what it takes to win?

What would you do in this scenario?

Imagine you're at a new job; you've been there for about two months. On your lunch break, you constantly bump into a colleague named Pam who comes across as very friendly, with a bubbly personality and quite smart. You immediately take a liking to her and start opening up about your life.

It's now three months into the friendship and she actually ends up being one of the most negative people you've ever met. She's ultimately looking for someone who's only interested in her daily negative drama. At some point in the three months, you told her that becoming a doctor was your ultimate dream and you're ready to take the necessary steps.

Pam, 'your friend,' tells you that you're not qualified and your goal is impossible to achieve; that you need to focus on your priorities in life versus focusing on unrealistic fantasies. She tells you that we all have dreams but let's get real.

If somebody like Pam really existed, wouldn't you want that person out of your life as quickly as possible?

So here's the interesting thing about someone like Pam – she lives in your head every day! If you won't let someone else tell you what to do, then why let negative thoughts lead the way? If someone who cares deeply about you heard half of what your brain said to you, he or she would probably tell your brain to F... OFF and leave you alone! Get my point?

If you're lucky, Pam might leave you alone for an entire day but sooner or later, she will revisit you, telling you how terrible your life is and to give up. The good news is Pam doesn't exist! The bad news is that if you're not serious about your vision or purpose, then I promise you Pam will appear to destroy your dreams. Harsh? Yes, but I had to learn this lesson the hard way; I would wake up every day and fight against the negative voices in my head. I had to fight for the things in life that truly make me happy. The clearer I became in life, the more Pam started to leave me alone.

DON'T LET FEAR PARALYZE YOU

Food for thought

If your dreams took 15 or 20 years to accomplish, would you be willing stay patient and remain determined to achieve your goal? If yes explain why? If no, then please reconsider what it is you really want to achieve in life.

Additional Notes:

"The way I see it, if you want the rainbow, you gotta put up with the rain."

Dolly Parton

Chapter Three
Courage

Having courage doesn't mean that you are without fear or apprehension. Many of us have acquired irrational fears based on past experiences and we talk ourselves out of doing things before we even begin.

Our desires in life can conquer our fears. If you desire something badly enough, you will find a way to go through it, around it, and over the fear in order to get to the other side. This is what courage feels like and this is what it's all about. When we doubt ourselves, we tend to look to others to make our choices for us. Yes, seeking advice is always helpful but if you're not careful, it could also be hurtful. Have courage; believing in yourself is key. Don't let others dictate your happiness or choices in life.

One of the biggest first steps you can take right now is to except who you are and whatever you want to do in life, flaws and all. When you hold on to this type of attitude, the opinions of others don't matter as much. It takes time and practice, but it's worth it. We're all worth it. Getting past your own fears and the opinions of others is a GIANT step in attaining courage. That doesn't mean you won't be afraid from time to time, as fear in some situations is necessary. The courage I'm referring to helps you get past the fears that only you know about. Think about it, nobody else knows, so why do you stop yourself from moving forward? When you truly start to Believe in yourself, the world will start believing in you too.

Read this again and think about the things that keep blocking you from moving forward, or ask yourself why you constantly tell yourself you can't have whatever it is you want in life.

List things in your life that you feel are blocking you from moving forward.

_____

_____

_____

_____

_____

_____

Now I would like you to list the reasons why you can. The "Why" is always what drives us and keeps us going. What is your driving force in life? Are you willing to muster up the courage and fight for it, or is it just something you truly desire? The best motivation is intrinsic motivation; it must come from within – it must be something that you personally desire or you simply won't have the drive to attain it.

Please list the reasons why you can achieve what you want in life.

_____

_____

_____

_____

_____

Once again, having courage is feeling the fear and doing it anyway. While we may stumble and fall at first, I promise that if you don't give up, the many rewards and lessons you will receive are all worth it in the end.

I would like you to write down below what your *dream life* looks like. "Whether you think you can or think you can't – you are right." – Henry Ford

_____

_____

...continue your dream life over the page

DON'T LET FEAR PARALYZE YOU

...continue your dream life here

_____

_____

_____

_____

_____

_____

Additional Notes:

"Twenty years from now you will be more disappointed by the things that you didn't do than by the ones you did do. So throw off the bowlines. Sail away from the safe harbor. Catch the trade winds in your sails. Explore. Dream. Discover."

Mark Twain

Chapter Four
Truth

What is truth? Truth is personal and subjective for each individual. We each have our own truth, and furthermore we each believe in our own truth. No matter what our cultural backgrounds or life experiences are, our truth is shaped by the people and our environment as well as the external forces in everyday life.

Whether we know it or not, whether we listen to it or not, the truth is that innate 'knowing' within that speaks to us in volumes at every moment. It's the visceral communication between our soul, our body and mind that guides us to do the best for ourselves and for those around us. Yet, some of us can't stand in our own truth when faced with opposing dynamics from our environment. When we let ourselves be misguided by those opposing dynamics, we sometimes get stuck or find excuses that let our fears rule our decisions in life.

Where does our truth come from?

Truth cannot be defined because our truth has been shaped from birth by our parents, schools, peers, friends, lovers, the media and more. All of these external forces have taught us to believe that our truth is real. Yet, there's no way to prove that anyone's truth is really right or wrong.

I believe the truth of humankind should be governed by respect, compassion and love in order to salvage the human race. We all have our teachings and differences but with human values and compassion, we can understand and respect each other's diversity and personal perceptions.

The art of communication or dialogue is becoming less important and obsolete through social media and today's technology. Our human communication is becoming more and more compromised and disconnected, which is why people are suffering more and more every day.

Why does our truth matter?

Our truth allows us to stand up and face our challenges with integrity, dignity and self-respect. Standing in your truth gives you the courage and strength to deal with any manipulation, lies or adverse obstacles that may come your way.

How do we come to trust ourselves –how do we come to believe in our truth?

The best way to start trusting ourselves is to gain the courage to keep trying to achieve our goals and aspirations. Whether we have been tainted or suffered in the past, we can choose differently by learning from our experiences. By making these new choices, we end up proving to ourselves that our past sufferings no longer reinforce our negative thinking.

Try and use your past challenges as opportunities to make great changes in any area of your life. If you can make the effort and do this, you will also discover your authentic truthful self.

Metamorphosis of ego-self to your naked-self

How do we change our perceptions to make new choices in life? When we embark on the journey of change, the process will inevitably come with some great challenges. As you become immersed in your development, you will begin to peel off the layers of illusion that have been your false security for years. Stripping away your personal ego or definition of self will not be easy, for with every layer that is peeled, you will probably experience some sort of grieving, sadness, vulnerability and even anger.

When you allow yourself to become fully connected to your naked-self, new challenges may be presented to you that may want to take you off your path.

Keep in mind that when you open up and allow yourself to become vulnerable, the process can be very difficult and even painful at times. Be kind to yourself when starting the journey. The essential component is giving yourself permission to open up and process your truth.

Cocoon

It is only you who must choose to go through the metamorphosis. You must experience the death of your old habits and behaviours, attachments and limitations before you can experience your true life.

When you finally stand completely naked in front of the mirror and see your true reflection for the first time, you allow yourself to become connected to a new vibration that is yours to discover.

Freedom

Our human nature makes us want to soar and discover more in life, or learn more about what life has to offer. When your ego-self ultimately dies and you completely shed the false shelter of your cocoon, you will discover your true purpose or mission. Trusting this human intuition allows us to disconnect from old frequencies and patterns and expand our lives.

Have you ever heard of the Chaos Theory? If not, I recommend you look it up. The term Butterfly Effect is a synonym for Chaos Theory.

Here is an excerpt about Chaos Theory and the Butterfly Effect from Wikipedia:

"Does the flap of a butterfly's wings in brazil set off a tornado in Texas?"

DON'T LET FEAR PARALYZE YOU

The flapping wing represents a small change in the initial condition of the system, which causes a chain of events leading to large-scale phenomena. Had the butterfly not flapped its wings, the trajectory of the system might have been vastly different."

We affect everything around us. And if you need proof, it's been scientifically demonstrated that the simple experience of observing something changes the very thing being observed!

What do you feel is your Truth? How have the Chaos Theory and the Butterfly Effect set off a chain of events in your life?

_____

_____

_____

_____

_____

Additional Notes:

"In my country we
go to prison first and
then become President."

Nelson Mandela

Chapter Five
The Truth Shall Set You Free

As innocent children we have nothing to compare life to; it's usually the time in life when things are easy and effortless – a time when our minds aren't consumed with jargon, fears and outside influences. This is such an amazing period in life; there is nothing to fear and we operate from a place of purity. One thing I know for sure is that the feeling of being absolutely pure with no preconceived ideas is truly one of the best places to be.

The feeling after a white lie

My first white lie took place when I received my report card for the very first time. Grades and report cards weren't high on my list as a child; I didn't care if I got an A or a D. Truthful enough?

So it turned out that I didn't do so well in school, which was reflected in my report card. When my mother saw my grades, she wasn't impressed. She explained the importance of school and how I needed to listen to my teachers. I had not done my best and felt horrible about it. I promised her that I would do better the next time around. My problem was that I couldn't keep my mouth shut in school and only cared about making forts and running around with my classmates. Well, sure enough, my grades were even worse on my next report card.

Then came the day that completely changed everything. I bumped into another little boy who had also not done well in school. When I asked him how his parents reacted, he told me he had lied to his parents about his grades and told them there would be no parent/teacher meeting this time round. I was in complete shock and couldn't understand the notion of lying to your parents. Once I understood what this lying thing was, you better believe I sure as hell came up with a brilliant excuse for my second report card.

As young as I was, I came up with a brilliant story and told my mother that the teacher's meeting had been moved to the following week, hoping that she would forget. Guess what? She did!

So yes, I got away with it. I had avoided getting into trouble (at least, for the moment), but let me tell you that the next day, I felt as if I had committed a crime. I kid you not. I remember feeling guilty and ashamed because of what I had done to my mother. It felt like the bond we shared had been completely broken and there was no turning back. I don't know how else to explain it; it was weird. The feelings I experienced were horrible and I promised myself to never lie to her again.

How valuable is your truth?

Being honest and living in truth is, in my opinion, the best gift you can give yourself. When we resort to telling a lie, it's usually because we don't feel worthy within the given situation. Yet if we strive towards the truth, I believe our lives can and will open up into a state of peace and pure acceptance. When we're fully in rhythm with the universe, the forces of life start to collaborate and support us on a different frequency.

Our unique personal make-up as human beings is absolutely spectacular. Trying to redefine our natural state or authentic self is pointless. We're all destined for true greatness in life and we must allow ourselves to strive towards the things that ring true to ourselves. Your family, boss or even next-door neighbors may disapprove of your decisions but ultimately your truth is the only thing that should matter.

Truth is powerful, truth is necessary; truth can make a difference in the world. Running away from it doesn't necessarily make you a coward, it just means that you'll leave this planet with an incomplete life and the world will never experience the fullness of who you truly are.

Your true mission in life

Is it too late in life to accomplish your mission? In my book, the answer will forever be no, it's never too late. This applies to everyone reading this. It doesn't matter how old you are, this book is a reminder that if you stay on your path and believe in yourself, your real truth will eventually show up. We must not let our doubts prevent us from what we're truly meant to do in life. If your truth means quitting your job or telling someone not-so-good news, then so be it. I'm not advising you to be irrational about your decisions; what I am saying is to be wise about your wishes in life and take the appropriate steps towards your goal.

Now's the time

Stop procrastinating. Get up and tell yourself every day that you're worth it. Life is not a board game – it's real and it is yours. It's your real life that will lead you toward your happiness. You have control over the choices you make; you can shape your life so that it leads to your given destiny. This, my friends, excites me every day: knowing that I face my fears. I used to be extremely hard on myself and never gave myself enough credit. I came from a place of doubt and fear and that prevented me from living a great life. When I realized I had been doing this to myself, I had to face the truth to find my truth. I learned that by being honest and expressing myself, I was becoming the type of person I wanted to be in the world.

DON'T LET FEAR PARALYZE YOU

What are some doubts you feel are preventing from achieving your goals?

_____

_____

_____

_____

_____

_____

Starting today, what can you do differently?

_____

_____

_____

_____

_____

_____

Additional Notes:

_____

_____

_____

_____

_____

_____

_____

_____

_____

_____

_____

_____

_____

_____

_____

_____

_____

"In seeking happiness
for others, you will
find it in yourself."

Unknown

Chapter Six
Responsibility

We often underestimate how much responsibility comes with making certain decisions.

Many of us are waiting for an outside force – be it a person, religion, or even a support group – to guide us towards our happiness. The truth is that it's all up to us. I believe in asking the intangible forces for help, but I also believe that support will come when we take 100 per cent of responsibility into our own hands. At the end of the day, we all cultivate our own happiness.

For as long as I can remember, I knew that I had to be the change in order to see my life manifest the dreams that we're circling in my mind. Think about what we can accomplish when we stay interested and learn the lessons of life. If you take responsibility, apply the lessons and never give up; you'll soon realize how powerful your life is.

Responsibility is a gateway to happiness

Finding your happiness and taking responsibility is a part of building a solid foundation. In my experience within the entertainment business, my whole life has been surrounded by agents, managers, business partners and more. Deep down inside, I realized that I'd been dependent on them and expected them to be responsible for the type of career I desired. When I stopped and thought about the business I chose, I quickly understood that in order to survive in anything successfully, you can't wait for people to be more responsible for your success or happiness than you are.

A key component in taking responsibility is to first become clear. Make sure you have a full grasp of the different outcomes you want in life.

If you can't take full responsibility for your life, there's a very good chance that you won't be able to maintain the many levels of commitment and happiness you are envisioning for yourself.

I keep trying and things aren't opening up for me. Am I taking full responsibility?

No matter what career you choose, no mentor, boss or best friend can outline your future. This is where self-reflection comes in; only you can figure out the missing pieces of the puzzle in your life. Sure, people can help – or paying people a pretty lump sum can solve your immediate problem for a short period of time – but the truth is that only you can make the significant choices.

Here's an example of someone who wants to advance in life but is in a toxic platonic relationship. In this scenario, Bob needs to take responsibility for his life.

Sally starts a business relationship with Bob but he soon finds out that Sally wants more than just a business relationship. She tries to force the situation and suggests that they should be together for the rest of their lives and even have children. What should Bob do? Should he walk away and forget the business? Or should he focus on the business and try and work it out with her? Some of you may say get the hell out of there; others may advise that he stay focused on the business and work through it by having a serious discussion with Sally.

Whatever option you chose, remember it's not always so black and white. The real question is up to Bob. Since he made the decision to go into business with Sally, he needs to take full responsibility to either walk away or stay. Not easy in the beginning, but when we're forced to look a certain situations honestly, we can surprise ourselves with how we choose to deal with them.

Give yourself a pat on the back for making it this far

Responsibility comes in several forms. The everyday responsibilities of taking care of our bills or family are things that people don't often congratulate themselves for achieving, so I'm congratulating you today. Congratulations and thank you for fighting every day to stay alive and making ends meet. Some of you are students, parents, teachers, seekers – whatever your position is in life, be proud of your personal achievements.

Self-reflection

This section requires some sort of soul-searching. I'm not saying you have to go to a mountain top and escape from the world to get in tune with yourself, but I do recommend that you start to visualize how you can truly make a difference in your life.

Try it today and see what happens. Please be patient with yourself and practice, practice, practice.

In the example above, what would you do if you we're in Bob's shoes?

_____

_____

_____

_____

_____

"The most beautiful people we have known are those who have known defeat, known suffering, known struggle, known loss, and have found their way out of the depths. These persons have an appreciation, sensitivity, and an understanding of life that fills them with compassion, gentleness, and a deep loving concern. Beautiful people do not just happen."

Elisabeth Kübler-Ross

Chapter Seven
Breaking The Chains

How many of you feel hopelessly stuck in life?

At one point in my life, I realized that if I didn't remove the shackles that were limiting me, I would end up facing dire consequences. I'm talking about high levels of stress, depression, anxiety…even suicide.

What do I mean when I refer to chains?

Chains refer to the pain or past situations that you haven't dealt with; the shackles left hanging. I use the term chains for all the things in life you keep avoiding.

For example: Have you had 'the' conversation with your father and told him the ways he hurt you growing up? Have you confided to your best friend about what's really bothering you? Did you cheat on your girlfriend? Are you sexually frustrated and in the closet? Are you feeling guilty about something and need to speak to someone about it?

Whatever the chains look like to you, make sure you're ready to be honest with yourself and stand your ground. Let's not fool ourselves anymore - the chains I'm speaking about are the ones that may need some time to process and get through. If you have to take your time and slowly chip away at them, so be it. There's nothing more exciting than to remove the chains that bind you and make peace within.

Getting to the root of the problem

At a certain point in my life, I got the urge to speak to a medium. To be honest, I had never been interested in that kind of stuff but decided to open myself up and dive into unanswered questions. A trusted source told me I should try it and see what comes of it. So I did.

One of the first psychics I saw told me there was a curse in my family that needed to be removed. Call it whatever you want, but when she told me about the curse, a sharp pain immediately went through my body and I started to sweat. I'm telling you, it felt so real that I almost fell out of my chair. The only way I can explain it is that I had always felt a heavy weight in my family and never knew how to truly explain it.

The medium offered to remove it for me, but I knew deep down that I would be able to take care of the situation myself. Even though there were times I wasn't sure what I was doing, I knew I had to get rid of the so-called curse placed upon my family. After doing some research and speaking to trusted sources about the issue, the first thing that made sense to me was to start with myself and look at the situation directly in the face. I started with a food cleanse, then meditated and chanted for the heaviness in my family to go away. The overall experience helped me look at the root of the problem and I took care of it myself.

Did any of this help me?

Yes, 100 per cent. The deeper I got, the better I started to feel. Clearing up the stuff that made me feel heavy or confused eventually led me to the other things in my life I needed to clean up. Sometimes the answers are right in front of us, other times we need to search for them.

My determination to be happy is truly something I desire and want in this lifetime. I made a vow to myself that I would do whatever it took to get to a point where I was no longer holding on to any negative feelings in my life. If I feel like anything is bothering me, I look at it, use wisdom and be honest about it, whether it's my health, career, family or relationships.

This doesn't mean you have to seek out a medium to clear things up; it just means that you need to recognize the shackles and work on whatever it is that may be holding you back.

Running away from life doesn't help anything. Substance abuse, lying to yourself or any other type of escape catches up with you when you least expect it. In my case, whenever a situation of stress comes up, I use the power of faith or exercise to keep me focused. Trust in your own power and you too can truly activate and manifest the strength you need to keep going.

What have the chains done to you?

_____

_____

_____

_____

_____

_____

Write down what your major chains look like? Be open and honest. Are you willing to remove the chains that bind you?

_____

_____

_____

_____

_____

_____

"The only way that we can live is if we grow. The only way we can grow is if we change. The only way we can change is if we learn. The only way we can learn is if we are exposed. And the only way that we are exposed is if we throw ourselves into the open."

C. Joybell

Chapter Eight
Don't Run Towards The Obvious

When I say don't run towards the obvious, I mean that your life doesn't necessarily have to align with the rest of the world. Being conventional works for many but being unconventional can also work too. However you choose to live your life is essentially up to you. I like this chapter because it reminds me of the rebel we all have within us – someone who takes risks, someone who's not afraid to try something different or new. Being paralyzed in life is no way to live; we're not only fooling the people around us, we're essentially fooling ourselves. Allow yourself to explore, live and learn.

I always tell people who feel misunderstood by those who can't see their vision, to say anything at all. Trying to defend your future with people who don't understand you is just not worth it. I don't think it's their fault; they just can't grasp your truth. They're usually the people who project their own personal fears into your life and encourage you to do 'the right thing' or 'the safest thing.'

The way to cope with being misunderstood in life is to work hard and make something out of yourself, then go back and share all of things you've accomplished with the people who couldn't see or understand your vision. That way, you leave no room for discussion or disappointment because it's already done. Make sense? It's all about timing. Remember that sometimes it's not wise to discuss your vision with anyone. Do your life homework, get clear and make it happen.

DON'T LET FEAR PARALYZE YOU

Have you ever felt misunderstood? If so how?

_____

_____

_____

_____

_____

A pivotal moment in my life

I was visiting my mother in Montreal when she told me someone had left me a message about an audition for a new television show. I had just returned from a contract in Paris and my body needed a break.

After listening to the voice message and job description, my first reaction was that what they wanted from me wasn't at all part of my life plan. However, I felt I should at least look into it. "Who knows, you never know what this new opportunity can bring into my life," I thought. So I decided that perhaps it was time to try something new and different. After a series of auditions, I ended up booking the TV show called Dancing with the Stars (Francophone version) and had a wonderful time working with the cast and crew. After a brilliant season – and having the time of my life – I reflected about the things that were most important to me. I thought deeply about the show and what my next steps should be. It wasn't an easy decision but in the end, I decided to terminate my contract and follow my gut intuition.

Once I made my decision public, my peers as well as the show's producers, fans and friends couldn't understand why I would want to leave. My intention wasn't to offend anyone; I just knew I had to move on in order to strive towards opportunities in different parts of the world.

At the time, people thought I was crazy to walk away from a successful television show, but looking back, I realize it was one of best decisions I ever made in my life. Not running towards the obvious was risky, yet completely satisfying at the same time. The amount of twists and turns I've made with my life since then has been astronomical.

It's worth it in the end

At the time, my life looked a little like this: I had walked away from a successful television show just after purchasing a new home and didn't know where my next job was coming from. On the flipside, in my heart it felt like I had made the best decision for me.

After leaving the show, I moved to Vancouver to further my career. With time to reflect in beautiful B.C., I came to the decision and wanted to start my own company called ANU Entertainment www.anu-entertainment.com. After four years in Vancouver, I followed my heart and moved to the Los Angeles area in order to study filmmaking.

Making these huge steps and taking a huge leap of faith is a level of trust that only a few will truly understand. If you can develop that level of conviction within yourself, then there's no way you won't succeed in what you want to do. Again, it may not be what you planned initially, but eventually it works out in the end.

Building trust within

The greater forces in life still amaze me every day. No matter how crazy the situation may feel at the time, something outside our human control comes into play and takes over. The protective forces are always there – you just need believe in them and trust that everything is going to be okay in the end. The only way to experience something like this is to take the risk and jump. If you continue to take the same path even though you know deep down inside what you should be really doing, then you will forever live in the land of fear. You will never witness the beautiful complexities life has to offer.

Leadership

Was it easy for me? No. Was I determined to be happy? Yes. Everyday I wake up and know the journey has just begun. Once you've sacrificed, fought, persevered and proved that you can do it for yourself, the congratulations and celebrations in life will soon start to appear.

When you're not running towards the obvious your a stronger leader. When you hold onto to the truth within, your leadership skills will quickly develop into experiences you can't even imagine. Whether you're going to the bank with a business plan or trying to prove to your boss that you deserve a raise, only you know what's best for you. Only you can plant a seed that will eventually blossom into something truly amazing. Please remember: if the seed takes time and effort to grow, don't get frustrated and impatient with yourself. Let it take the time it needs. Don't let frustration, lack of patience or boredom stop you from doing what's necessary. If you're not willing to invest the time for yourself, then nobody will.

Warren Buffett, one of the richest men in the world

I don't know him personally, but I highly respect Warren Buffett's humility and focus. When I started to learn about the human being behind the money, I became interested in his life and philosophy.

When we're given certain gifts or skills in life, we must pay attention and cultivate them into something great. In Buffett's case, even though he describes himself "Born a privileged caucasian boy" with a father who supported his endeavors, he didn't take his privileged life for granted. Buffett learned that the most important things in life don't always include money. He likes money but doesn't let the idea of money control his nuclear family. He knew that if you want to be successful, then you have to work smart to get there. Yes, Buffett knows wealthy people and does business with them, yet he still remains humble.

At the age of seven, Buffett already knew what he wanted to do in life. By the time he was 11-years-old, he bought his very first stock market share. Was his father a huge influence? Absolutely! Yet, to be so clear at such a young age is a gift. As an adult, Buffett quickly learned not to be swayed by other people when making business decisions, even if the stock market was unstable.

With a net worth of $75.6 billion in 2017, Buffett was listed by Forbes Magazine as the second richest man on earth, following Bill Gates. The real beauty behind all of this is that Buffett believed in himself and stuck to his beliefs from a very young age. If you're able to plant those seeds when the stock seems down and reap the benefits when it goes up, that, my friends, is true victory. If Buffett did not have faith in his decisions – had he simply moved with the masses – he certainly wouldn't be where he is today.

Are you willing to believe in yourself?

Your belief system has to be like no other. Again, just because people around you don't understand your every move, that doesn't mean you're going in the wrong direction. When you plant a solid tree in life, it's going to take time to mature.

It's like watching the Dragon's Den, a television show about ideas, entrepreneurship and conviction. People with ideas, or small business owners, try to convince executives that they have come up with the next new thing, something worth investing in. The beauty of the show is that you can tell right away if the person facing the Dragons has just come up with an idea or if he or she has been working on their project for years. Neither one is better than the other; it's all about preparation, along with confidence and knowledge about what they are trying to sell. The ones who knock it out the park are the people with a belief system like no other. When your mind is made up and you know what you want, I believe you will achieve the best outcome in life.

Fundamentally, not running towards the obvious doesn't mean you have to be perfect and ready to go. It means that you're able to look beyond the regular things most people do and go for it anyway. Your way.

It's not just about fulfilling our dreams

One of the things I've learned is to follow your heart no matter what people may say or think of you. Think about it; we only have one chance to do and say what we want in this lifetime. You not only have to prove it to yourself, but you can also help the person next to you.

If you can impact another person's life while improving your own, the reward is absolutely phenomenal. Taking yourself out of the equation and knowing that you're doing something right automatically makes you a hero in life. Helping people is truly underrated; when you can get past your own stuff and help another person see the greater good in his or her life, you will feel very happy that you did.

List 10 ways you can avoid running towards the obvious

1 ....

2 ....

3 _____

4 _____

5 ....

6 _____

7 _____

8 ....

9 ....

10 _____

Additional Notes:

"Let us all set our sights on leading great lives dedicated always to truth and move toward that goal in good health, brimming with hope. Let us live our lives bodily, without regret, advancing with patience enthusiasm and a genuine spirit of friendship and camaraderie."

Daisaku Ikeda

Chapter Nine
Never Give In To Other People's Insecurity Or Jealousy

This chapter is dedicated to all the bright lights who constantly dim themselves so that they don't ruffle other people's feathers. Sidestepping what you believe in or what you want to do is the last thing you should worry about.

Are there good people out there who believe in your version of happiness?

Yes, absolutely – but it can take time to build a healthy circle of friends. Whether we're independent individuals or not, our support system can help us through the most difficult times. Do whatever it takes to build a solid circle. If you don't have one, then build one. Make sure you find people you can depend on.

What do you mean by never giving into other people's fears or jealousy?

We need to stay focused on trying to achieve our goals in life. Be careful that you don't get stuck in someone else's insecurities or fears. Whether people are doing it intentionally or not, their advice may affect your future decisions. Always remember that at the end of the day, it's your life and not theirs.

DON'T LET FEAR PARALYZE YOU

Success can be tricky when things start to work out for you. It's not always obvious at first, but when that certain somebody smiles in your face but has ulterior motives, you need to watch your back and open your eyes. Jealousy is nasty and sometimes we don't see it right away. The only thing you need to be concerned with is your end results. No one else but you should decide your future. No one.

Some of you may be blessed and know exactly what you need, others may need years upon years to figure it out – and that's okay too. Just be wise and take care.

Make a list of the people you think don't serve you well.

_____

_____

_____

_____

_____

_____

NEVER GIVE IN TO OTHER PEOPLE'S INSECURITY OR JEALOUSY

Write down how you've let some of their insecurities and jealousies impact your life.

_____

_____

_____

_____

_____

_____

"It's not whether you
get knocked down;
it's whether you
get back up."

Vince Lombardi

Chapter Ten
Authenticity and Compassion

Authentic behavior is one of the best ways to move forward in life. To experience a real, raw, beautiful connection on every level is what I think every human being should strive for. Whether it's platonic or romantic, nothing beats having a real connection with another human being. The world would be so much better if people could leave their egos at the door and be themselves.

It's always incredible to witness young children without filters – they possess an authentic point of view, and there's something beautiful about that. Often as we grow older, many of our innocent and beautiful qualities get lost along the way.

Sincere and genuine behavior

Sincerity or authenticity often results in earning respect or genuine love from the people around you. They know what to expect and can appreciate the real you. No tricks or games are needed to win people's love, just being the real you is more than good enough.

What is compassion?

Having compassion means you've recognized another human being's feelings or situation. You've made a connection and understand what the person is going through.

The key to embody compassion is to sincerely step into the other person's shoes. We obviously don't exactly know what the other person has gone through, so we should take the time to really find out where that person is coming from and just listen. Try to hear them out before you hold on to a negative thought. Yes, many of us do have similar issues or problems in life; however no two people will live identical lives. When I actively listen to someone, I remind myself that the person is not me and that he or she is facing their own challenges. I recently read that the obstacles we face are put in our laps to help us evolve into happy people. It's not a matter of what happens to us it's how we handle the obstacles. If our goals were easy to attain, we would have already attained them. A goal is only a goal because of the challenge. So, before you go ahead and judge someone, remind yourself that their current battle is as real to them as whatever struggle you're facing in your own life. This is huge. When we have the ability to break down barriers and build connections, we're able to communicate and bring light to any given situation.

If you have problems with someone, compassion will help you put your issues aside and see the person for who he or she really is. Step out of your own perceptions and opinions and try and connect with the person in front of you. If a person can put ego aside, the situation immediately shifts into something purposeful and then things can begin to heal. When we hold on to negativity, it harms everyone.

Another way you can be more authentic and compassionate is through the efforts you make towards your personal development. Aiming toward a higher level of consciousness helps you handle the things that continue to show up in your life. Once you are living consciously, you will become the kind of person who not only speaks up for yourself but also for the people around you. Injustice to others is injustice to you or your family. If it doesn't feel good to you, chances are it won't feel good to someone else.

Compassion really is the greatest gift in this world; it is the core of humanity. Seriously, we all need to take care of each other. Our compassion needs to be extended to those beyond our immediate families and social circles. When we can see others not as separate or distant entities and understand that we are all just people with different opinions or feelings, the world will become a better place. We can then create a healthy environment through love and acceptance.

Judgment

Judgment is one of the biggest barriers to compassion. Try to embrace a person by holding love and understanding in your heart and then see how your relationship changes.

Empathy

Empathy is defined as the psychological identification with, or the vicarious experiencing of the feelings, thoughts or attitudes of another.

An empath is someone who can connect on a deep emotional level with another person. These people are said to be able to experience what another person is feeling emotionally. Sympathy, on the other hand, is sharing a feeling with someone. That usually happens during times of sadness, grief, or despair. Nevertheless, both empathy and sympathy are about having compassion.

Because it's right

What do you do when no one is watching? What would you do if you found a wallet chock-full of cash and no one was around? Situations like this test our integrity. When I was a kid, the question was "do I keep it or give it back?" As an adult, it's no longer a question. Of course, this goes back to treating others as you would like to be treated. For example, if you lose your wallet, it not only means losing the cash value, it means having to cancel all your cards and replacing them. What a hassle!

Do you try to get away with things or do you try and do what's considered 'morally correct.' It's never too late to start making better choices. Imagine how great the world would be if we all functioned in this manner.

Giving and receiving

People have different levels of comfort when it comes to giving and receiving. Studies have shown that people with a lower sense of self-esteem tend to be more comfortable with giving than receiving. Those who love themselves are usually equally comfortable with both giving and receiving. If you're someone who doesn't receive well; gifts, compliments, favors, or help, ask yourself why? While the gift definitely is in the giving, nobody should be uncomfortable to be in the receiving position. You should never have to give anyone anything to be friends with them and if you find yourself in this scenario, please reconsider how real you're being with yourself.

Instead of asking yourself why others aren't doing more for you, try asking yourself what more could you be doing for them.

A disconnected world

Reconnection begins with an actual connection, which is what many of us have lost in today's world. Put the technology down and go see a friend or family member. We're out of touch with one another because we're physically out of touch. We always justify it with our busy schedules. We all seem to live separate lives but we need to find a way to come back and reconnect with one another.

Here's my take: do what you can to make your world or environment a better place. Hopefully, your influence will be infectious and the next person will want to do the same.

When we help others, we're essentially helping our own personal growth and evolution. There's something about the power of giving; you end up walking away happier when you witness others benefitting from your support and compassion.

Intuition

To me, intuition is simply, truth . It's the part of you that just knows and follows what feels right. We tend to get stuck in a very scientific, pragmatic world that constantly wants and needs answers. Unfortunately, most people have become somewhat out of sync with their own intuition.

When you choose to stay disconnected and only use the rational part of the mind, you can only go so far. Your intuition tells you everything that you need to know; you just have to learn how to trust it and let it guide you.

False fronts and insecurities block our inner guidance. When you become quiet on the inside, you can hear the guidance that you need to follow.

Once you've cleared up what's blocking you, you can then ask yourself the important questions.

When was the last time you felt a strong pull or calling to do something? How in-tune were you with your intuition?

_____

_____

_____

_____

_____

_____

How do you begin to differentiate between what you should or should not follow?

The more honest you are with yourself about absolutely everything, the louder the messages get. It gets to a point where your intuition can't be ignored. Intuition and authenticity can be used in so many ways, including helping. It can help you relate to others. – Compassion, on the other hand, is all about understanding and relating to others. Your intuition knows what you need to do in order to truly be happy. It may not always be understood right away, but trust your own personal guidance regardless. People who are highly intuitive can also hone in on the emotions of others, which makes it easier to understand them.

The next time you get a strong feeling to do something and you can't find a reason why, do it anyway and see where it takes you. Your life will become layered with incredible experiences.

If I look back at some of the unexplainable things I've done, it amazes me to see the great things that I've achieved. Trusting my intuition has made my life richer. Intuition has been one of my greatest gifts and continues to guide me in the right direction. I'm hoping your learn to listen and trust your intuition too.

The golden rule

We often hear that we should treat others as we would like to be treated. When I first heard this expression as a child, it made a lot of sense to me. I began to incorporate that motto into everything I did. The problem was that I was willing to treat others far better than they were willing to treat me. My logic was that if I treated each person with respect, then that's how they would treat me. I've learned, that's not always the case. You can easily find yourself being taken for granted if you go overboard.

How can I remain compassionate when I feel people are taking advantage of me?

First of all, are you willing to admit to yourself that you've been tolerating their poor behavior, staying angry and waiting for them to change? Or are you willing to stand up, develop courage and compassion and speak your mind? Which choice is more empowering to you? Many times it's about being the bigger person. Yes, it can be exhausting but sometimes it's the only way. It's easy to lose your temper when a person who is important to you knows how to push your buttons; you can either fly off the handle or choose to stay calm and assess the situation. The latter choice is the healthier of the two.

Treating others as you wish to be treated also includes being assertive and calling people out. If you're upfront, clear and honest about your feelings, then you definitely can come to a healthy resolution. We can sometimes get trapped with the idea that any type confrontation is bad and that the situation will end negatively. If we get calm within ourselves first and then approach the situation with wisdom, usually both parties will come to some type of agreement and walk away in peace.

If there's no exchange happening between two people, then someone in the relationship needs to stand up and make a healthy decision to either get help or move on. It's that simple. I'm not saying to give up on the person but if there is any sort of real suffering, someone has to make the best decision for the relationship.

Grace

Grace is one of the things I mention because it's very important. Find every bit of strength and self-control you have to be graceful with someone instead of losing your temper. Learn to respond instead of react. It's definitely a skill that takes time to acquire but practicing it is worth it. If you're a highly emotional person, know in advance that you will already need to possess a great deal of patience and emotional self-control.

Always remember to be strong and kind to yourself first! Walking around with a guard up in life doesn't change anything at all. People deserve your love; just make sure you are giving the love to the right person.

Ulterior motives vs. compassion

When you treat others far better than you treat yourself, people may question your motives. If you're doing things for others because you are coming from an emotionally needy place, people will pick up on it. It's human nature. If you're being genuine and have no ulterior motives, people will appreciate the gesture nine times out of ten.

You can be the difference

Believe it. You may think that you can't make a difference, but I assure you that you can. You never know what chain of events can be put into motion from just one action.

Start looking for new opportunities to practice compassion. If you open your eyes, there is a lot of kindness in this world. Good things happen every day. People out there are helping each other. Look for it. Many charities and groups exist to help others. Volunteer. Get involved!

You can create your own reality by choosing not to dwell on the negatives in the world; Notice and acknowledge them, be aware, but don't focus on them. I can assure you that there are many good things happening in the world. Attitude is everything!

What are some of ways you can practice compassion and make a difference?

_____

_____

_____

_____

_____

_____

Practicing compassion

By releasing pent-up poisonous thoughts, you'll more easily free yourself from any unhealthy situations. Changing your perception is one of the most powerful things you can do for yourself. To see it from another's perspective is priceless. The more people you begin to do this with, the easier it will become to practice compassion.

Can you think of any place where you could be practicing more compassion in your life?

_____

_____

_____

_____

_____

Look at your relationships with the people in your life, past and present. How can you show up differently with any of these people in ways that promotes understanding and healing?

_____

_____

_____

_____

_____

"Having the idea of being successful is easy, the work behind success never stops."

Michael Challenger

Chapter Eleven
What Are You Willing To Sacrifice?

The power to sacrifice and knowing how to change your situation is one step closer to your own personal victory. The self-discipline I embraced and sacrifices I made helped me through the toughest times of my life. Sometimes I navigated my ship in the open sea without any clear direction - yet when I became clear and made the necessary sacrifices, the universe always led me back on course.

No matter how you look at a situation, all of your experiences shape you to become the person you need to be in order to overcome life's challenges. You may not always like what you see, but you must be willing to look at yourself honestly and make the necessary adjustments.

Why do I have to sacrifice anything? I should be able to get whatever I want.

One of the biggest traps in life is not knowing when to let go. When we get stuck in a routine, we become victims of our chosen environment. Feeling entitled and not doing what's necessary for change, only reinforces your decision to stay in a stagnant place. When you feel like you deserve a better life but are not willing to do the work, it's very unlikely that you will receive any benefits either. To want something is exciting; to know your dreams won't manifest overnight is even more exciting. You may feel anguish, anxiety, or anger in the beginning but in reality, it's usually our ego or laziness that keeps us from achieving our goals.

I'm not only referring to extravagant things; I'm talking about the everyday material things that define who we are - the things we couldn't imagine ourselves living without.

Please identify and write down three of your bad habits.

1 _____

2 _____

3 _____

I want you to try and break those bad habits for two weeks – just two weeks, not one year. Try it and see what comes up for you.

If you can do this, then you can sacrifice the other things that are stopping you from moving forward. That's the point; we're using these tools to try and eliminate negative behaviors and feel proud of our accomplishments.

What are you willing to sacrifice?

Sacrifice is defined as something important or valued that your willing to give up for the sake of other considerations.

If you don't yet know what you really want, it can be hard to know what you're willing to sacrifice. Please make sure you give it some thought. When you've figured out what you want, then you'll know what you're willing to sacrifice in order to get it.

Take a spin on the word and make sacrifice a joyful decision so that in a few months, you'll be happier with yourself.

Sacrifice = Discomfort

The reason we avoid making certain sacrifices in our lives is because we often associate sacrifice with change and discomfort. The problem is we make this discomfort so much larger in our minds than it really is. It's so easy to talk ourselves out of doing something before we even get started! The truth is, once you begin to make small sacrifices, you'll find out that what you've gained has so much more value than doing nothing at all.

Temporary happiness

While there are certain material things we may need at times, in general these things won't bring lasting happiness. No one ever felt better about keeping up with the Jones's. Once you purchase that new 'thing', you'll eventually get tired of it and need the next thing. If you're on a budget, try to come up with some inexpensive ways to still have a good time and enjoy life. Getting lost in retail therapy or buying the new toy won't get you very far.

Let's face it; we don't really need half the things we purchase. Most of us live way beyond our means and don't even remember what we have. The next time you're in a convenience store, department store, or even a bar, try to visualize the end result and make the necessary sacrifice.

One way I can prove to you that sacrificing really works is to point out the type discipline it took for someone like me to stop moving around and write this book. I had to kick my willpower into gear and focus into shape and make it happen. Now looking back, I've never felt happier. When you say it, believe it and push through it, you will eventually see the results. If I never practiced what I preached, there's no way that you and I could experience this journey together.

Know what you want

If you're not sure what you want from life, taking the time to focus on your personal development is an important step forward.

To gain more clarity, try something new and completely different. If you need a place to start, think of a few options, experiment and give it a shot. You may come to some truths by trying out something that you don't want.

Forcing ourselves to make decisions when we feel confused or pressured is something a lot of people do because we don't have a choice. Very often, paying the bills and taking care of your responsibilities can push aside your ultimate dream. Just be sure to remain focused on that dream. It may take some time, but don't let it die.

Always remember, doing nothing changes nothing

If you want something in your life to change, you have to get up and change it. Theoretical knowledge is great, but nothing beats learning from the school of hard knocks. Over time, this will become a skill you can apply to any other part of your life. We all know this, but when will you be ready to actually do what's necessary?

What would you need to do to change things right now? If you don't do something differently, you know that things will ultimately stay the same. Is the change worth the improvement? Decide that you're ready to make the tough choices, figure it out and go get it.

Discipline

Discipline can be defined as an activity, exercise, or a regimen that develops or improves a skill. It's also considered a type of training.

Essentially, it's about following through. Think about the previous times in your life when you had to discipline yourself to do something that was important to you. How did you feel when you accomplished your goal?

Here's something I do that works for me: I change my routine almost every week because I tend to get bored easily, I change my routine almost every week. I cover the same things but not always in the same order; that way it stays fun and dynamic, which is what I like. What small change could you make each day that would change your life drastically over time? Change your routine to incorporate this new activity and discipline yourself to follow through.

Financial sacrifices

Take a look at the type of things you spend your money on. If you're not sure where you spend your money, I highly recommend carrying around a journal or taking notes on your phone for a few days. Track down all the purchases you normally make throughout the week. You would be surprised at what you habitually spend money on and how these things add up. Not getting your morning coffee or snack can save an extra $1,000 a year. That's a lot of money! What alternatives are available to you? Instead of purchasing a pricey cup of coffee each day, maybe it would be better to get yourself an espresso maker or some other high-quality coffee maker and make your own.

Relationships

Another type of sacrifice we all need to consider is maintaining our relationships with our significant other, family and friends. If you find yourself always making the sacrifices, then something is off-kilter. Be careful about what type sacrifices you make so that they are not only beneficial to others but to yourself as well. Exchanging life experiences is key. If your relationship is 100 per cent only your partner, you need to go back to the drawing board and determine what's best for you as well. Use your wisdom so that both parties are evolving in the same direction.

Is it worth it?

Make sure you have a strong desire to achieve your goal before you begin. Get to your core desire by knowing what's driving you. Know your WHY... this is your FUEL. You won't have the drive to go through challenges if you don't know why you're doing it.

When you can step outside of your own limitations, you'll see things more clearly. Sometimes it can be feel overwhelming but when you stick through it and put trust into your everyday actions, eventually you'll be proud that you stuck through it until the end.

DON'T LET FEAR PARALYZE YOU

What if I don't know how to go about it?

The person that succeeds in the end is the person who's willing to do the work. Gain some clarity and come up with a plan of action.

Which one of the following could you improve right now: discipline, financial, relationships. Explain how?

_____

_____

_____

_____

_____

_____

Additional Notes:

"Promise yourself to be so strong that nothing can disturb your peace of mind."

Christian Larson

Chapter Twelve
Reconnect With The Child Of Your Past

Children have the most amazing energy. Think about the last time you spent quality time with a child, whether yours or someone else's. They're so full of wonder and excitement about everything, it's captivating. Kids think about having fun and doing whatever their heart tells them to do.

The best part is that children take bigger risks than adults. Very often if things don't go according to our plans, we feel disappointed and give up. On the other hand, kids keep going and don't let the negative consequences stand in their way.

As teens, most of us worked at part-time jobs and we told ourselves we had to start at the bottom so we took any job we could get. Regardless of the job, we learned significant life experiences that shaped our future. Then time flies by and we forget about our dreams. We settle and become less content with life.

We are sometimes unable to make sense of what's missing, but we carry a void within us to adulthood.

Forgiveness

Think back to when you felt both safe and good. Hold onto that feeling. Consider how you feel now and the things you learned along the way, as well as the fears that you acquired. Bring the adult back and tell the child within you: "It's okay; none of those experiences are your fault. You did nothing wrong, you did your best at the time." Forgive yourself and release whatever pain you've been carrying; it's the best thing you can do for yourself.

Anger

Going back to the past can be a touchy subject for many people. It can be especially hurtful if you consider your past to be painful or a rocky road. The quicker you learn acceptance, the less difficult your past may seem. Accept what happened and work on moving on from it.

Are you hanging on to anger from your past?

_____

_____

_____

_____

_____

Can't figure it out?

Sometimes it can be hard to figure out things about ourselves because this is not an area in which we can always be objective. If it was that easy, everyone would have figured it out by now. I look at how I've interpreted things from the past, take what I've learned since then and try to look at the situation somewhat objectively. By doing this, you'll understand what needs to be processed so you can let it go. Only then will the emotional wounds begin to heal.

A traumatic childhood can leave our inner child wounded, confused and hurt. Although usually carefree in nature, children often feel that the bad things that happen to them are only happening to them. Anything that makes a child feel different from his or her peers is surely something they will go out of their way to keep secret.

Did you have a traumatic childhood or know someone who has? Have you told anybody about it or received help? Were you or your siblings abused? Maybe your parents were never home and often left you alone. Maybe when you where a kid, blaming yourself was all you knew how to do; kids don't know any better. Blaming themselves for things that go wrong in a family is unfortunately, very common. They draw conclusions based on their small worlds. If you blamed yourself for something as a child that you now know wasn't your fault, you've already discovered how unhealthy this can be. Looking at a past situation with newfound awareness can help you grow tremendously. If you did experience some type of abuse, trauma or neglect as a child, please keep in mind that most likely, you were not the only one to go through an experience like this. Regardless of what it was, help is out there. There are groups for almost every type of human experience or addiction – you just need to know where to look.

It's also possible that you remember being unhappy as a child but have no idea why. Simply accepting that you've been miserable for a long time and not knowing why is a lot more empowering than denying your misery. Realizing this simple fact alone might encourage you to make changes in your life.

Believe again

Creation begins within the imagination. Your imagination is only limited by the belief system that you've created for yourself.

As a small child, what did you believe was possible that you no longer believe to be possible today? Is it something you still want? If so, have you considered what it would look like and are you up for it? Try to believe in miracles again.

DON'T LET FEAR PARALYZE YOU

What did you believe was possible as a child. Please list below:

_____

_____

_____

_____

_____

_____

Merging the child and the adult you

It really doesn't need to be one or the other. The child and the adult co-exist inside, because they're both a part of what makes you, you. Connecting with your inner child can improve your life in so many ways. You will begin to feel more complete. Your life will start to have more meaning, wonder, and excitement. Maybe your childhood dream is something you're no longer interested in pursuing. The best part about life is that you can always make new choices. So, if you wanted to be a school nurse because you like kids and you like to help people, but now you're selling houses and hate your job, what new choice can you make today? What would the little boy or little girl inside of you tell you to do? Changing course is always an option. Decide to honor your inner child. No need to go on punishing the little one inside you anymore! Love them fully, with complete acceptance.

Write down the best qualities you possessed as a child and how you can apply those qualities in your life today.

_____

_____

_____

_____

_____

_____

"Belief in oneself and
knowing who you are,
I mean, that's the
foundation for
everything great."

Jay Z

Chapter Thirteen
How Much Love Do You Give Yourself?

Many of us have vowed to love someone else for the rest of our lives, but why can't we make that same oath to ourselves? Shouldn't we fall in love and get married to ourselves first before loving another person? I would love it if we were first taught how to love ourselves before loving anyone else. I believe, the world would have less warfare, less divorces and less hate.

Self-love is not something that is taught in school or in society. Most people don't actually love themselves fully; we work, we get by in life and do what we need to do. But if we operated from a place of love, our lives could be completely different. When you signed up to share your life with another person, didn't that person initially fall in love with your unique qualities, dreams and desires? In the beginning, didn't that person tell you how much they loved you for who you are? For whatever reasons along the way, sometimes life experiences and situations creep up and we don't hold on to the things that most matter to us.

In my opinion, love is one of the most beautiful and yet complicated emotions things that exists on this planet. Love can build us into fascinating people with fascinating experiences or, if you let the power of love disappointment you, it can turn you into a very ugly person. Regardless of how you look at it, the power of love is pretty fascinating. A great friend of mine said to me one day: "I'd rather stand in love than fall in love." I found that very interesting and it has become one of my main mantras.

Using love as your weapon

It may sound cheesy, but I believe that love transforms anything and everyone. If you're comfortable with yourself and send love to the people around you, you'll be surprised how much it will enrich your life as well as someone else's. Remember, love isn't about being naïve, it's about developing wisdom in your life and using it in a powerful way. Think about what you can do with this type of love. It's truly amazing.

I sometimes hear of CEO's doing great things for their staff; throwing parties, inviting them to retreats and more. Being able to show gratitude to the people who've helped you become who you are is amazing. When people are acknowledged and obtain a sense of validation, everyone – including the CEO – is better off at the end of the day. Yes, I'm speaking to you hard-shelled folks; if you believe that showing love isn't the way, try it and see what happens. You'll be happily surprised.

In the Dickens classic a *Christmas Carol*, Mr. Scrooge gets a second chance in life. This is a great example of learning how giving back make others, as well as yourself, happier.

Be honest with yourself

Once you learn how to love yourself, you can unlock the mysteries of life. Being able to disconnect from the everyday noise and tap into your self-love is both powerful and exceptional.

The route to happiness is often circuitous. If you believe there's only one way to your chosen happiness, I rarely say this, but you're wrong. The more we grow and develop, the more we can understand that there are various types of happiness.

Here's an example of someone I know who's not willing to commit to loving himself

A friend of mine suffers from anxiety. He's currently in a situation where he's not happy living in North America. He thinks people here are too individualistic and have zero sense of community. He comes from a small village in Spain where people are friendly and share real struggles with each other. Is he right? Maybe he is, maybe he's not. The question is, how does he cope with his stress and anxiety in his new environment? I'll tell you how: he drinks 10 to 15 cups of coffee and smokes two packs of cigarettes a day; he drinks a lot over the weekends and feels like crap the next day. He hardly exercises and hates his body image. Now, I'm not a doctor or in a position to criticize the choices he makes, but this question keeps coming up in my head: how much can a person possibly love himself with that type of lifestyle?

Another scenario

I was speaking with a beautiful friend whom I've known for 15 plus years – long enough to really know a person. She had a problem finding the 'right' man. She was bawling her eyes out. "I can't take it anymore. I just can't take how evil the people are around me are. Why is the world so corrupt?"

After a long discussion, I plainly said to her: "Stop being so hard on yourself; nobody is making you miserable. You've made a very clear decision that you no longer want to fight for your life anymore!" Surprisingly, she agreed. I told her that it was time to start being responsible for her choices and start loving herself. "No man, or anyone for that matter, can truly make you happy." In tears, she said: "I don't love myself; I'm old, ugly and nobody loves me." Was she on the pity-potty? Hell, yeah! Does she have the right to be on the pity-potty? Hell, yeah! But how long do we actually stay on it? If you're not willing to love yourself from the inside out, the cycle will never end.

The incredible thing about the power of loving ourselves is that we can build the lives we want to live. By working through our own pain, we not only enrich our lives, we also shine light into someone else's. No matter what your past looks like, you're here for a reason and it's your job to find the things that work best for you. Don't let negative forces take over! Don't ever let anyone tell you different; never run away from a situation, no matter how hard it may be at the moment. Take the time to discover the love you have inside you. Don't dismiss or begrudge your happiness; understand its power and use it to the best of your ability.

During my life I've been lied to, cheated on, manipulated and more, But I can finally say I'm happy and love – truly love – all of me. This is why I'm ready to give back in life. If you've been abused, lied to or cheated on, try working on getting back to who you really are. Using the pain as an energy force to move forward in life is the way to go! It took me years to understand all of me, years to cultivate and find the tools to make me happy. I found the right formula and I'm still learning. It never stops. We all need to sit down and have a civil conservation with ourselves.

Not every example in this book will make sense to you. Trust me, I get it. Loving ourselves is profound. We've all developed ways to escape and cope with life when our pain comes up.

Write down the things you love about yourself?

Additional Notes:

"When life and the world continue to send you messages, don't take it lightly, pay attention to what keeps coming up."

Michael Challenger

Chapter Fourteen
Staying Open In Life

Staying open in areas where you most likely need to change is probably one of the hardest things to do. Rebounding back into a comfort zone can feel good temporarily, but you're going in the wrong direction. The goal is to move forward.

Staying open to possibilities is one of the key components I learned in changing my life.

Benefits to being open

My own fears in writing this book couldn't have been overcome without staying open to change, without having the will to continuously evolve. I couldn't have started this book had I not been open and willing to face all the necessary steps to advance in life.

Staying open requires a lot of patience and some risk into uncharted territory. When you start to advance and feel happy, you may notice that some people in your life may change in accordance with the new life choices you've made.

I will always stay open no matter what life presents. It's not always easy, but people teach you something about yourself everyday if you stay open and don't ignore the signs. What you can learn and discover is astounding. Some of the best people and things have come into my life because I was open. Not one of those experiences was a waste of my time.

Staying open to life means so much – it means you've tapped into a place of peace and strength within yourself. That place allows you to accept whatever it is that's going on around you without feeling you have to control the situation.

Staying open also means holding on to a positive attitude. It's amazing what a little courage and vulnerability can do to advance your success. Essentially what I'm saying is to have faith in whatever your heart desires, stay open and walk towards it.

Being open and letting go of the pain

My father and I have never been close. Is there a problem with that? No. Did I want things to be different growing up as a child? For sure. Was he around for any soccer games or significant times in my life? No he was not. Could I understand that as a child? No, I could not. Was I angry as a child? Yes, I was, for a very long time.

But when I sat down as an adult and thought about the truth of my father, I realized that he was young and made mistakes in life, just like everyone else. Should he take responsibility for his actions? Yes. Does he deserve to suffer based on the things he's done in the past? That's not for me to decide – that's for the universe, God, the mystic law, whatever you want to call it, to decide. I can't hold him accountable for the rest of his life. But I can stay open and develop a new relationship with him by being accessible to the person he is today. Staying open to challenges and working through the feelings of anger can truly change your experiences in life.

When I remained open to my father's life experiences, I listened and I learned. I discovered and saw a man that hasn't healed from his own past traumas, a man who's still stuck in a place of suffering, pain and guilt – a man who's stubborn for all the wrong reasons. When I made the shift to stay open to his life and see him as a regular man, it set me free from the anger and pain for which I had held him responsible. It allowed me to release the expectations of what I thought a father should be – and it was one of the best experiences in my life. I now can simply respect him as a regular man, with imperfections.

Being open has also taught me to love a person no matter how much pain he or she has caused me or others.

There's no time to waste

By simply observing and learning, I continue to grow and understand that our life on this earth is too precious to squander and waste time holding grudges or getting stuck in other people's stuff. Let alone your own.

The challenge is to remind yourself that the evolution of life is never-ending; we can't expect to stay open for only a day and shut down for the next six. Setting yourself free and working towards your happiness is an ongoing process. Whether it feels good or not at the time, we must continue to believe and make the necessary shifts. The more open we become, the clearer we are on making decisions. The bigger the mission in life, the more we must be clear and teach others around us.

What can life look like when you allow yourself to be more open?

If you've blocked yourself from certain situations because you've been too afraid to express your feelings, the best thing to do is open up just to prove to yourself that you can do it. We're all capable of letting go and moving forward to bigger and greater things. By doing so, we develop our own power and strength, which leads to personal fulfillment.

When we step outside the darker parts of life and seek greater things, only rich experiences will come. It is then that we will be able to cultivate the things that are most important to us.

It is important to continue to grow and understand what life has to offer. The more open you become, the more you will experience and receive. When we carve out a glorious life full of adventure, happiness, laughter and strength, we can be thankful every day. Every day is a new beginning so please continue to stay true and open to what life has to offer.

DON'T LET FEAR PARALYZE YOU

Please write down ways you can be more open

Additional Notes:

"You are the average
  of the five people you
  spend the most time with."

Jim Rohn

Chapter Fifteen
Unlimited Power

What excites me the most about all I've learned so far, is that we each have the power to change and the power to redefine our lives.

I felt the power when I was younger but I didn't yet fully understand how we can manifest whatever we want or need in life. The protective forces within the universe have been unbelievable. When you're clear about what you're meant to do, everything aligns to supporting you.

When we stay open in life and tap into our individual gifts, things start moving in a way that only a few can understand. When we ask, we shall receive. That simple? Yes. It all depends on how badly you want to see the change. The clearer you become, the clearer the manifestation.

I always thought I had a secret power as a child. I believed that I could manifest everything I wanted. I was already tapped into something greater than I could possible imagine. They're no coincidences. If I had understood half of what I know now, my life might look very different.

Facing difficulties

We sometimes think that bad things happen only to us. "Why did Pam get the promotion and not me?" "Why can't things flow easily so that I can just be happy in life?

Try flipping the script. The thing that pisses you off in life is the very thing you need to look at and investigate. Why is it happening to you? Look at a given situation and see it as an opportunity to grow. We learn to understand that life challenges are gifts too; it all depends on how you react to the obstacle.

Who defines our power?

As an artist, I would often take workshops with teachers or coaches to help support my growth within the entertainment industry. One of the exercises we did before starting the workshop was to face each other – people we had never met before – and shout out the first occupation we visualized them doing in life. (By the way, you could try this exercise with friends, but the best results come from doing it with strangers).

The objective of the exercise is to learn how people view you in life versus how you see yourself. This exercise is usually done with actors but I believe it can work well with people who are looking for a new path or feel stuck. If anything at all, it gets the brain going. My process was very interesting. I got hit with several types of occupations: a lawyer, a pimp, a doctor, a nurse, a cop, a designer as well as car salesman. The process completely changed how I saw myself and taught me that I could be anything I wanted to be. It taught me that it's never too late to re-examine what you've built by reconstructing the components of your life. It's truly an amazing exercise. If you're a teacher, try it with your students – it can truly open up their minds and help them view themselves differently.

What you'll discover behind your unlimited power

Unlimited power comes right back to the real you. There's no point in trying to connect with something that doesn't represent you or doesn't feel right.

Your power is incredible and if you allow it, everything within the universe will guide you towards the bigger picture. Believe me when I tell you that I had no desire to be in the entertainment industry. I'm not even quite sure if I knew what the life of artist looked like; it was completely out of my psyche.

But being open even at the age of 13 changed my entire life. Entering into the world of arts has been absolutely mind-blowing – the things I've learned, the people I've met. No words.

Remind yourself who you are

The process of getting to know yourself or reconnecting with yourself doesn't mean you have to cut your hair off and fast for thirty days – but if that's something you want to do, then go for it! All I'm saying is take some time to be alone and have some quiet time with yourself. Pay attention to your wants and needs and assess the things or voices – those gut feelings – that keep coming up. I discovered my power through meditation and chanting. When I started to connect and understand the power of my inner self, I was transformed by taking the time to heal and took charge of my personal life. I discovered the real and true essence of who I am and my real mission in life. It accelerated my process in life and helped me become a better person. But again, that's me. If you've figured out ways that work best for you, that's great. You're the CEO of your life.

Some of you have been blessed to have parents or mentors who helped you along the journey and gave you direction. But for those like myself, I had to learn life through observation and by seeking out different ways to become a better human being.

What excites me about our power – your power – is that no one, absolutely no one, can take it from you. You were born with it, it's yours to keep and no one should tell you how to use it.

Concern yourself with your own unique power and let the people around you discover their own

I'm very protective of the lives of the people that I love and of course, my own. No matter how bad a person may seem to be, he or she has the potential to become a wiser, better person. If they get the opportunity to learn and grow from their mistakes, allow them to grow into something beautiful. We often point our fingers at other people and expect them to be a certain way. Instead, take the time to focus on your own stuff and live by example.

The truth is that everyone operates on their own timetables. No matter how much you know a person and his or her potential, sometimes they're just not ready to take the leap and change.

DON'T LET FEAR PARALYZE YOU

Set the people you love free

At one point in my life, if I saw potential in someone, I would go beyond my capabilities to help them change. But I finally realized that some people don't want the help – a huge lesson for me! Listening to someone compared to enabling them is completely different. They are responsible for finding their own power within themselves.

There are so many rewards in store for you when you take a good, honest look in the mirror. Even if you've made mistakes , it's okay to shake it off, do better and work on developing the power of your goodness within. Try to start your day knowing that you can change your circumstances – whether it's debt, a broken relationship or your dreams. There's nothing holding you back; there's always hope and power within the universe to support you.

If you feel someone trying to take power from you, re-evaluate the situation. You may be giving it away.

Please write down what personal power you possess.

_____

_____

_____

_____

_____

_____

Additional Notes:

"If strength is what you seek, then stay open enough to fail along the way."

Michael Challenger

Chapter Sixteen
Having No Doubt

When we doubt ourselves, we are subconsciously telling the universe that we're not ready. Unfortunately, when we hold onto doubt, we suppress the many opportunities life has to offer. Of course, like anything else, a healthy amount of concern means that you care about what you're doing. But if you let the doubt continuously stop you from moving forward, it can become a serious problem. Doubt equals fear. Plain and simple. The goal is not to let fear paralyze you, remember?

So, Before you continue to read this chapter, I want you to look at the doubts that are preventing you from moving forward.

List 10 reasons why you doubt your ability to achieve your goals

1 _____

2 _____

3 _____

4 _____

5 _____

6 _____

7 _____

8 _____

9 _____

10 _____

Doubting our abilities to see who we really are can come from not being able to see or control the future. Our inner critic can be so strong that we give up on our dreams because nothing at that time seems promising or worth it.

The power of taking a step back and looking at the situation objectively offer a better insight into the things that don't always seem tangible.

Ways to eliminate our doubt

Being clear about eliminating your doubts and not being ashamed or embarrassed to ask for help is key in setting yourself free.

Believe it or not, most people want to help if they see you're serious about achieving something.

Gaining confidence doesn't come from sitting around doing nothing; it comes from getting up and confronting the things that may take you down.

Doubt is completely subjective but being confident is a decision. Doubt can produce massive doses of fear. We must face the fear, the doubt and overcome.

Determination

Our determination in life can overrule and conquer anything. Getting past our own fears and the opinions of others is a giant step in attaining control and happiness. Once you are determined, you will come to a clear resolution of what you want and no longer want.

Do you have a strong burning desire for something specific?

Please list below what your determined to achieve.

_____

_____

_____

_____

_____

_____

Insecurity

Are you afraid of something in particular? Whatever it may be, it is possible to change. You need to feel confident in your abilities if you are to succeed at anything. I used to tell myself I didn't have any fears, but I wasn't being honest with myself. I had my own fully stocked arsenal.

With time and practice, I began to feel more confident. Like all great things, becoming a secure person is something that takes time. I'd rather fall on my face a few times to get ahead than stay stuck in mediocrity or discomfort. Sometimes when it gets to be too much and we (temporarily) give up, this is exactly when the answers come to us. This is because we were too emotionally involved or charged to make any further action possible. When you let go, you can reach a higher plane which then makes a physical manifestation possible.

Self-esteem

Self-esteem is everything. Do you feel that you are a person who deserves to be loved and respected? Are you worthy of all the best things the world has to offer? Do you feel respected by those in your life at work or by your friends and family? How well do you treat yourself?

You can usually tell who has a healthy amount of self-esteem. These people don't seem to be easily affected by the opinions of others.

Try paying attention to the people with whom you interact. See if you can tell which persons have a good amount of self-esteem. It's not about judging people; it's an observational exercise to help shape your existence.

Choice

Everything is a matter of choice. You're not predestined to be anything or anyone other than what you choose. And you can always choose to change your mind.

We tend to tell ourselves that we can only do certain things based on our past experiences. Just because you chose to be one thing doesn't mean you can't choose differently now. It's okay if you were in one field and are now contemplating changing to an unrelated line of work.

Sometimes our train of thought keeps us stuck in a place where we don't need to be. Getting ideas from other people can be quite helpful. Keep making choices. If past choices didn't work out well, try making new ones.

Forgiveness

Take another look at the main reasons why you feel stuck or are having trouble moving forward. Are you the kind of person who beats yourself up for making mistakes or do you tell yourself to remember it, learn from it and move forward? I do the latter now. In the past, I would beat myself up about something I did wrong – and I would carry it with me into new experiences. All this did was cripple me. I still have to remind myself that I am not my mistakes.

I am not my mistakes

Whether you are holding on to negative feelings about yourself or someone else, you're only hurting yourself. If the pain you're carrying is towards someone else, ask yourself who's really hurting. The other person may not even be aware of your feelings.

Remember, a new moment is happening right now. Let go of all the perceived wrongdoings of the past and choose to move forward. It's hard to look ahead when your eyes keep looking back. Just let it all go and keep going.

I will no longer be angry with (insert your name here)**. I will move forward starting today. (Repeat as often as necessary)**

Please list five people you are willing to forgive (Including yourself)

1 _____

2 _____

3 _____

4 _____

5 _____

Perseverance

What happens if we give up? Nothing. Nothing happens. Nothing changes. Perseverance is crucial in order for growth to occur. Tell yourself: "Whatever it takes."

Being able to complete your goals despite the challenges that may arise is a true sign of perseverance. Keep going after your goal no matter what happens along the way

Overcoming doubt and turning it into confidence

If you don't recall a confident moment in your life, look at those around you. Can you differentiate between who is confident and who isn't? It's not hard to tell. Most likely the confident ones are striving to accomplish something better for themselves in some way. Make the choice to overcome your own doubts and perceived limitations.

Can you think of the times in your life when you felt confident? Maybe it was at a job you loved, or when you used a particular skill? Maybe you took a martial arts class or played an instrument you loved? Whatever it was, think about it now. How did it feel to be confident? Did you feel that way when you first started out or did it take a lot of effort, time and practice to get there? I'd bet you also had to make sacrifices along the way.

_____

_____

_____

_____

_____

_____

WINNER'S CREED

If you think you are beaten, you are;

If you think you dare not, you don't;

If you like to win, but think you can't,

It's almost a cinch you won't;

111

DON'T LET FEAR PARALYZE YOU

If you think you'll lose, you are lost;

For out in the world we find success

begins with a person's faith; It's all in your state of mind.

If you think you're outclassed, you are;

You've got to think high to rise.

You've got to be sure of yourself before you can ever win a prize.

Life's battles don't always go to the faster or stronger hand;

They go to the one with faith and always think "I CAN."

– Walter D. Wintle

Additional Notes:

"When you smile,
the whole world
smiles with you,
but when you cry,
you cry alone."

Stanley Gordon West

Chapter Seventeen
Self-Sabotage

So many of us lead busy lives and can't seem to get things in order. We're caught up with family, friends and work. Sometimes the things that most matter to us get pushed aside. Why is that? Why don't we do the things we know could help us?

When I used to think about the steps I needed to take to become successful in my career, I would outsmart myself by doing nothing at all. I just pushed it aside.

The more I thought about opening up to write this book, the more fear would fester inside me. I'm sharing this with you because one of the main reasons I wrote this book was to overcome my own fears. The longer it took to write the more I realized I was preventing myself from helping other people. I went deep within, looked at the patterns in my life and wrote down the things that I needed to change. I didn't feel like I was progressing fast enough for the mission or dreams that flooded my heart every day. I would think about it 24/7, 365 days a year and didn't see any results. It wasn't enough for me and I needed to do something about it.

Any of this sound familiar? Have you ever been a victim of laziness or been afraid and pushed your dreams aside?

DON'T LET FEAR PARALYZE YOU

Please list the ways in which you continue to sabotage yourself.

_____

_____

_____

_____

_____

_____

Get out of your way

Self-sabotage can be so sinister that you may not even be aware that you're doing it. You may have plans to do something or you might have even started the process, but you continue to put things on the back burner.

Here's the thing: self-sabotage can come in many forms. Underneath the facade of self sabotage lies our enemy, fear. The most important thing is to remove the road blocks that get in our way.

Here are a few common road blocks

Common blocks: I've always had the dream of accomplishing (fill in the blank) but I don't have enough time to get it done.

First, be rational and honest with yourself. Does attaining your dream require less play time and less zzz's? Most probably. Does it mean more planning and research? Absolutely. The type of commitment you need to make in order to fulfill your dreams has to be like no other.

Common blocks: When people ask why you're not on a patio drinking sangria, you'll know why deep down inside. Things don't usually happen overnight and your now committed to a dream-there will be plenty of time for Sangria.

116

Common blocks: I'm too tired and don't think I have the energy to fulfill my dreams.

This is when we have to be honest with ourselves about what we're fighting for. Stop fooling yourself by letting fatigue get in the way. If you're tired, then you'll never survive in the wilderness. As a leader, you always have to come back to your core inner strength when striving for greatness and reaching your goals. The last thing anyone wants to hear is: "I couldn't accomplish my dreams because I was too tired."

If you're waiting for an outside source to take care of your dreams or problems, it will never happen. You need to wake up with drive, start your day and take action.

Write down all the road blocks your going to eliminate

_____

_____

_____

_____

_____

_____

"Not forgiving someone is like drinking poison and waiting for the other person to die."

Anonymous

Chapter Eighteen
The Public You Versus The Real You

Who doesn't want to gravitate towards the things that make us feel good and comfortable? It's only normal that we lean towards the things that work well for us in life.

For most of us, something happened along the way – whether it was at school or work or even at home – that made us think it wasn't okay to fully be ourselves.

Hypothetically speaking, let's just say that there was an incident in your family that made you feel like you didn't fit in or that you were misunderstood. Feelings of being unaccepted among family or friends can be emotionally crippling at a young age and can literally affect your entire life.

Children generally do what they have to do to be accepted even if that means agreeing with things they really don't want to do. At a young age, most of us are consumed with being accepted rather than with being authentic and real. Some of us grow out of this stage of conformity; others continue to live a public persona and hope to fit in.

When you wear your auto-pilot survival hat, the people around you may think and believe you are being real. Over time however, we end up creating a persona that is no longer manageable or viable.

Living a lie doesn't work

When we hide behind lies and deceit, we eventually start to lose the game called life. Trying to hide or fit in doesn't serve anyone, especially when trying to deal with real happiness.

When we hide and try to please the people around us, it's not only exhausting, but it doesn't eliminate the pain from growing. The saddest part is that whatever it is you're keeping to yourself is most likely covering up an incredible person, gift, talent, or skill.

Real friendships or relationships

Real relationships don't start from ulterior motives or lies. They start with organic connections that grow into something special, and the rest is history. When things are organic and not forced, the more honest and deeper the friendship becomes.

Of course, any basic relationship can be enjoyed for a certain period of time, but eventually you'll know whether that person is going to remain in your life.

Are you brave enough to be yourself? Therapists sometimes call it, 'peeling off the onion.' Once you've made the acquaintance of someone new and know that this is a person you want to have in your life, the relationship will eventually reveal itself. You both will know where you stand. If you're coming from an authentic place, people will feel it.

Extremely trustworthy people make the best of friends because they're people with integrity and respect. If the person you're trying to connect with is hiding behind lies, you'll always feel unsatisfied with the relationship. When lies are used to convince, sway or bribe someone, that person is usually setting him or herself up for a failing relationship that will naturally reveal itself. Real progress starts when natural chemistry develops between two people; you feel safe enough to let down your guard and begin to build and trust. As long as both parties are being themselves, the onion process starts to naturally peel. In getting to know each other, you can usually sense how genuine a person is being while having a conversation - the more open and honest you are, the safer the other person feels.

Let down your guard

Real progress in any type of relationship starts when you feel safe enough to let down your guard down and trust. There's always a chance of getting burnt but that's a risk we all have to take. Without risk, how can we truly benefit from the relationship and learn from the life experiences we need to grow in life? If one person isn't being real, it will definitely hinder the development of the relationship.

Use your intuitive radar to know which friendships are worth investing in and which aren't. For the most part, it's about starting to trust yourself and your choices. Once you trust yourself, it will be that much easier to know who else you can let into your life. The important thing is being able to count on yourself and to remain authentic along the way.

Being able to count on yourself is a major premise of this book. This is how strength, confidence, and courage are developed. By letting our guards down, we're able to let in those people that deserve our love and trust. If they break the trust you give them, you must be strong enough to let go and surround yourself with people who deserve the love that you give and share.

There's just ONE you

Differences are what make this world such an incredibly beautiful place. Imagine how boring it would be if we all looked and exactly the same? In essence, that's what we're doing when we're not being ourselves. You are unique in every way! Although the world has almost eight billion people in it, not one of them is just like you. Why would you ever try being like someone else and not celebrate your own radiant light?

If you're still a bit stuck, try and get over yourself! If you try to be less sensitive about certain things, then you can come to terms with your wonderful uniqueness and in fact, take great pride in it.

We spend so much of our time trying to change or fix what we look like or who we are. We obsess about having the perfect body, looking young, having the right job, making enough money and so forth.

In this obsessive type of society that demands perfection, how much life are we actually living? If loving ourselves really did come first, we would never put ourselves on such torturous quests. A goal should be a goal because it's something that makes you feel good and is worth doing. Your personal motivation should be the driving force behind your goals.

Be brave. Even if others aren't courageous enough to stand up and be themselves, you can be their inspiration. When people see you living from your truth, you will inspire them to do the same. Being courageous is contagious! Shed your cocoon and start being real. We tend to be our own worst enemies and biggest critics. When we play up our weaknesses and downplay our strengths, we just end up hurting ourselves by playing small and staying small.

Comparing yourself to others

Comparing yourself to anyone else is fruitless since there's always going to be someone better or worse off than you. Once you have come to love and accept yourself, the comparisons will stop. When you choose to focus on someone who appears to be worse off than you, then you are trying to make yourself feel better. When comparing yourself to someone you perceive to be doing better than you, it's because you're choosing to feel bad about the things you haven't achieved in life. There is such a thing as looking at people that inspire you to become better, but make sure you don't fall into the trap of jealousy or envy. Try asking yourself why and make sure to keep yourself on track and in check.

Comparing yourself to others is a gigantic waste of time. You are on your own path and that person is on his or hers . When you start thinking that they know more or are better than you, then you fabricate thoughts within that can't actually be measured. Yes, some of what you're thinking may be correct but in actuality, you may possess something that they don't have. I used to assume that everyone knew more than I did, and it constantly left me feeling that I was at a disadvantage. Even as a child in school, I remember times where I wasn't sure about the teacher's instructions and I would look around the room to see if anyone else knew what they were doing. Obviously, I should have raised my hand and asked for clarification but because I was too afraid to be yelled at for not listening, I opted to keep my mouth shut and try and follow along as best I could.

If you're always comparing yourself to someone you think has it better than you, then you're experiencing jealousy and/or envy. We all experience these feelings sometimes. If you're experiencing a negative feeling about someone else's possession of something you'd like to have, how do you think the universe reads that?

Being inspired is totally different from being envious or jealous.

Jealousy is being afraid to lose something. Envy is wanting what someone else has. In both cases, it's about someone else. What about you? Don't get distracted by trying to be better than whoever it is you admire; get through the test by challenging yourself to become better each and every day.

Pay attention

Part of being real is being strong and keeping your eyes wide open. Living in the present and always being aware of what's going on around you is crucial. I'm not saying you need to be perfect; I'm saying we should strive for improvement.

We're all trying to grow, evolve, and better ourselves. Actively engage in conversations with others and listen to what they're saying as they say it. Just continue to listen. Don't think about what you will say next. Now is always the only real moment that exists. It's always now. It's never yesterday or tomorrow or later. It's NOW. This will help you become a much more solid person, more present and aware of others.

Fake versus real

Lies are what keep people apart and the truth brings us closer together. Ask yourself what you're more interested in – staying separate or coming closer together? Opening yourself up, paying attention and not comparing yourself to others is essential. If you can let your guard down with others, you make it easier for people to get to know the real you and create a place of comfort in honesty. Very often, people are afraid to be exposed and unaccepted. When you open up first, you set the tone.

Once again, you can't get very far with anything based on lies. We've all heard the saying, "No pain, no gain!" Whether this statement is completely true or not, many of us haven't gained in life without experiencing some sort of pain. New levels of awareness will surely bring you new experiences. Each fear that you conquer will take you to a new place.

DON'T LET FEAR PARALYZE YOU

My eleven keys to being real

1. Be okay with imperfection. Nobody is 100 per cent perfect.

2. No one's opinion is more valid than your own.

3. Validate yourself. Love yourself. Approve of yourself.

4. Release attachments to people and things. Attachment = Control.

5. Be strong enough for those who seek to challenge you.

6. Trust yourself and your choices.

7. The choices you make need to be in alignment with your moral values.

8. Face fear head on.

9. Care more about what you think and less about what others think.

10. Be independent.

11. Find a mentor or person in your life for inspiration.

Additional Notes:

"Lots of people want to ride with you in the limo, but what you want is someone who will take the bus with you when the limo breaks down."

Oprah Winfrey

Chapter Nineteen
Freedom

The ability to be free and make your own choices in life is absolutely wonderful. The question is: how free do you actually feel in your life right now? Is your life consciously created by your own design or is it full of limitations?

Freedom is a choice for most people in life. You have the freedom to do what you want, so please wake up and run toward the things that allow you to be free.

What does complete freedom feel like for you? Please answer below.

_____

_____

_____

_____

_____

_____

Hard or easy

Who wouldn't love to just wake up each day and spend 24 hours doing what they love? Have all the money in the world. Go anywhere, do anything, travel to foreign countries and experience new things. I know I would. It would be amazing.

Our attitude determines how we view things in life. Do you wake up each day feeling excited or do you dread getting up and hate your life? Personally, I've learned that you always, always have to push through life no matter how tough it gets.

I've had some really rough patches in my life, but I understood that every single time I decided to smile, face the fear, choose freedom and embrace my life, I would walk away feeling happier about my situation and the people who surrounded me.

It can be really hard to wake up with a smile when your environment isn't what you want it to be. The thing is, feeling bad about something won't change it. Are you willing to work hard to feel free? The two go hand-in-hand. How much is your freedom worth to you?

Challenge yourself

Whether it's time, money or love, none of those things will actually fall into your lap unless you allow yourself to be free and welcome the gifts that life has to offer. Most of us cower when presented with a new challenge.

When was the last time you accomplished something that you seriously wanted? Think about how good you felt. After some time has passed, look back and remember how you did it and how great it felt.

List some of your greatest accomplishments so far

_____

_____

_____

_____

_____

_____

Try to remember a time when you envisioned something for yourself and your experience was even better than the picture you had in your head. Has that ever happened to you?

Life is all about creating balance. Give and take. Push and pull. Input and output. Risk and reward. You're going to get whatever you're willing to put out. You're basically investing in yourself, which is incredible. Stretch yourself. The only way to become big enough for your goals is to expand your life. A vast majority of people only do what's obvious and easy, but that's not always the answer.

Things in life that now feel impossible can eventually become possible. You may even begin to realize that in the long run, the obvious or easy things in life are anything but easy! If it's easy now, it may become more difficult down the road. Don't be so quick and run for a quick fix.

Maybe right now you're not someone who would appreciate the happiness you seek. It's quite possible that before you can actually enjoy your dream, some internal changes need to be made.

You want to grow, right? Then you have to be a bit different than everybody else and find true freedom and gratification.

Why don't I feel freedom?

Sometimes we don't realize that we've locked ourselves inside our own jail cell. Maybe you've put too much pressure on yourself and feel boxed in with nowhere to go.

On the bright side, maybe the reason you feel the limitation on your freedom is because you care. If you didn't care, you would just walk away from your responsibilities, right? So what options do you have? You can change the situation, or you can change how you see the situation. Did you always feel this way or is this a new feeling? What happened to incur this change in you? Has this been coming for a long time? If you're long overdue for a life change and unhappy with your situation, ignoring it will only make it worse. Please address it. Try to choose another option and see the situation differently.

I see so many people miserable in their jobs, day in and day out. It seems that over time, people become numb to their situations. Yes, needing money to live is the reality of life, but it doesn't have to feel like you're living in hell.

Make your life experience whatever you want it to be. Just because you can't see the light at the end of the tunnel right now doesn't mean it isn't there. Know that you have the power to change and free yourself.

The feeling of freedom

It's about how you feel inside. A person could be sitting in prison like Nelson Mandela did and still feel free inside. On the other hand, someone who feels like he or she is attached to a dead-end job is in a prison. Get my point? It's all about your state of mind.

After freedom

Once you've achieved a new level of consciousness, a series of new experiences will start to come your way. There is no limit to how much you can achieve once you start to believe that you can accomplish anything.

Moving forward

Please review all the exercises we've done together in this book. If you skipped any, go back and revisit them. We've all read books and learned so many fascinating things, but how many times have we actually applied the lessons to our own lives and did something about it? Simply reading won't cut it. You need to do the work and take action!

Actual change will happen through the combination of reading this book and completing the exercises.

Being able to count on yourself is a major premise of this book – how strength, confidence, and courage are needed for true fulfillment in life. True freedom is being yourself in every given situation. Without taking a new risk, there's never any real reward. It's time to redesign your life, go out there and just do it!

"Your dreams will
always defeat reality
if you give it a chance."

Anonymous

Chapter Twenty
The Next Level

I've created some additional exercises to further help you on your way. Hopefully, you've answered all the questions in the earlier chapters and done the work. Some can be done daily, others are a one-time thing. Decide which exercises help you the most. Everyone will feel differently depending on where they are on their journey. **Choose ones that resonate with you.**

Meditation – DAILY EXERCISE

The benefits of meditation are well documented and countless. People who meditate become more grounded and reap many benefits. Without distracting everyday thoughts, we develop a peace within. Not thinking about the future or removing our 'self' from daily stress can be really difficult and that's where meditation can help. I've included interludes in this book to introduce and encourage you to interrupt your thoughts and focus on your breath.

Try starting off with five minutes a day and then gradually increase the time you meditate. If you can get up to thirty minutes or more, you'll start to really feel the power of meditation. I mediate or chant almost every day and it has changed my life for the better!

Journaling - DAILY EXERCISE

Writing is therapeutic and cathartic, especially writing about yourself; it's like talking to a friend who's always there for you. It's a phenomenal way to process your thoughts and work through them. It's also a great way to see where you've been and even where you're going. Journaling will help raise your awareness, which is probably the most important thing you could ever do for yourself. Start off with free writing for about 20 minutes a day. Keeping a journal also helps you see how far you've come. Many studies have been done on the healing benefits of writing. Journaling can also help you process your emotions.

Fear liberator – ONCE EVERY SIX MONTHS

Choose one thing you have always been afraid to do or try. I am not recommending you go and jump out of an airplane, but I would like you to choose something you've been afraid to do. It can be anything. The purpose of this exercise is so you can see what it feels like be on the other side of fear. Once you're there, it's amazing! The feeling of coming out ahead of something that scared you is the best feeling ever! Please choose something that doesn't involve risking your life, but is big enough to make an impact in your life. Once you do this, write down how you feel afterwards. If you choose a big enough fear, you will have had an incredible experience. You might even feel a release, which has been known to feel like a rush. After you've liberated yourself from your first fear, move on to another if you're comfortable. Keep going until you've completely liberated yourself!

Intuition fun - ANYTIME

One day when you have nothing better to do, simply go for a drive or bike ride, with no destination in mind. Let your feelings be your guide. Try not to rationalize or justify anything. This is a free-flow exercise. When you get to a red light or stop sign, sit for a moment before choosing which way to go. If you feel a 'pull' to go in a certain direction or to a particular place, please do. The purpose here is to get you in touch with your intuition. I can't tell you how many times I've done this exercise and ended up with good results. Your intuition is your inner truth. Make sure you write in your journal what your results were. If nothing happened, don't be discouraged. Your intuition isn't going anywhere; you can pick it up and practice another time. Keep doing this. It will strengthen your inner guide.

Action tracker - DAILY EXERCISE

Learning anything is a reward in itself, but learning alone won't move mountains. When is the last time you took action towards accomplishing your goal? Reading is great. Doing is better. Once a day, I'd like you to do something you wouldn't normally do and then write down the results. Again, this is an ACTION you must take. Taking the smallest step towards what you want counts. Doing anything is better than doing nothing at all. What action can you take today to get closer to what you want?

Pay it forward - OFTEN

In case you haven't seen the movie, Pay It Forward starring Haley Joel Osmond, Helen Hunt and Kevin Spacey, it's about a young boy whose teacher gives the class an assignment. Each student must do a random act of kindness for three people and then those people are asked to do something kind to three more people. What kind of Pay it Forward project could you put together?

A recent experience of mine

Following a business meeting, my colleague and I decided to go out for lunch. We drove to the restaurant and began looking for a vacant spot. After ten minutes of driving around, we finally spotted a man backing out of his parking space. Not only were we happy to find a parking spot, but the man got out of his car and gave me an all-day parking pass. I have to admit my defenses went up at first, but I soon realized he was only trying to help.

During our lunch break, we spoke about how amazing it felt to meet such a generous man and discussed ways on paying the gesture forward to someone else.

So now it was my turn! As we were leaving, I noticed a man who was about to pay for his parking spot. I stopped him and told him that I would give him the free parking pass on one condition: that he must agree to pass it on to someone else when he left the restaurant. He cheerfully responded: "Absolutely sir, thank you very much for this!"

DON'T LET FEAR PARALYZE YOU

I have no idea how many times that parking pass went from hand-to-hand that day, but the point of the experience was that it all began with a small gesture that put a smile on my face and then that of the stranger I met in the lot – and perhaps a few other people. A small gesture, yet extremely powerful at the same time.

Here a series of anonymous quotes that inspire me. I hope they serve to inspire you too.

Many people will walk in and out of your life but only true friends will leave footprints on your heart.

To handle yourself, use your head; to handle others, use your heart.

Anger is only one letter short of danger.

If someone betrays you once, it is his fault; if he betrays you twice, it is your fault.

Great minds discuss ideas; average minds discuss events; small minds discuss people.

He who loses money, loses much; he who loses a friend, loses much more; he who loses faith, loses all.

Beautiful young people are accidents of nature, but beautiful old people are works of art.

Learn from the mistakes of others. You can't live long enough to make them all yourself...

There is no beginning or end. Yesterday is history. Tomorrow is a mystery.

Today is a gift, that's why they call it the present.

"Working hard towards your dreams should never tire you. Fight for your dreams"

Michael Challenger

Acknowledgments

To my amazing mother and father: **Paulette Theresa Challenger**
                                 Noel Sylvester Andrews

To all of the **family and friends** who continue to inspire me, every day. Your love and support mean the world to me and I sincerely thank you from the bottom of my heart.

A huge shout out to the **Soka Gakkai International**. I'm so proud to be part of SGI and prove the validity of Nam-myoho-renge-kyo. Thank you Sgi, I love each and every one of you and many thanks to you Mr. Ikeda this book is dedicated to the organization of peace, culture and education. Forever Sensei!

A warm and loving shout out to **the ANU Entertainment team**, your hard work and dedication continues to blow my mind.

Thank you **Pathways to Publishing Academy** for supporting the vision of my book. Your support during this process has been phenomenal.

And last but not least, thanks to all of you for purchasing my first book *Don't Let Fear Paralyze You*. I truly wish each and everyone of you success, peace within, true love and happiness.

Peace and blessings to all,

Michael

"I will always stand up
for the underdog."

Michael Challenger

Biography

Born and raised in Montreal, Canada, this peaceful warrior's passionate curiosity and zest for life began at a very young age. Through spirituality, yoga, healthy eating and physical training, this "Challenger" spends his time on the planet becoming more centered and grounded every day.

Award-winning director/producer Michael Challenger has built his multi-faceted career through high energy, business savvy and goal-driven success habits. Michael approaches each artistic and business endeavor with a natural talent for innovative and uniquely creative ideas and concepts while consistently delivering first-class results and outstanding achievement. Some of his film work has earned Best Direction, Best Film and the Award of Excellence. In the events category, he also received the Best Bat Mitzvah Award.

As a triple-threat professional performer in the business since the age of 13, Michael's reputation is built on his versatility, exceptional talents, incomparable 'people skills' and unparalleled work ethic. His expansive resume covers a broad range of professional credits including all areas of theatre, dance, film, and television. His many successful accolades include major Broadway productions, U.S. and Canadian television series' and major movie network projects. These vast opportunities allow Michael to travel the world as a performer, teacher, director, choreographer and producer.

Recognized as a natural born leader and entrepreneur, his career path took a ten-fold giant leap in 2007 when he created ANU Entertainment. As the owner, executive producer and creative director of ANU Entertainment, this progression allowed him to carefully evaluate and reflect on the direction of the company while exploring its many options for potential growth and expansion. Honing his many skills and talents toward directing and producing, Michael continues to champion the expansion and transformation of ANU Entertainment's services and is deeply-rooted in its gradual growth strategy to become one of the leading production companies in the world.

For more information please visit www.michaelchallenger.com or www.anu-entertainment.com.

Manufactured by Amazon.ca
Bolton, ON